COACHING HIGH SCHOOL FOOTBALL

A Brief Handbook for High School and Lower Level Football Coaches

PERRY GILMORE

Coaching High School Football / Perry Gilmore

1st Edition Paperback: June 2013

ISBN 10: 1-936185-84-9
ISBN 13: 978-1-936185-84-9

Cover Design: Laurie McAdams

Interior Design: Roger Hunt

Published by Charles River Press, LLC
www.CharlesRiverPress.com

Readers may contact the author at:
coachingfootball@usa.com
customerservice@charlesriverpress.com

"Perry Gilmore has done a wonderful job of giving aspiring high school coaches the basics of the game of football and how to coach it. If you are new to coaching, this is a must read."

—Steve Hunt
Managing Editor, Los Angeles News Group

DEDICATION

To my parents John E. Gilmore Sr. and Janice B. Gilmore: Thank you for your love, praise and discipline; and your correction when I needed it.

ACKNOWLEDGEMENTS

To all of the high school and lower level coaches who coach and teach football not for vain glory, but in anonymity out of love and respect for the game.

ONE
THE BASICS

The basics of the game of football are quite simple. There's blocking, tackling, running, throwing, catching and kicking. There are eleven men on the field for each team at any given time.

The team with possession of the football is considered on offense or on attack. The mission of the offensive unit is to progress down the field by executing a series of plays (called downs) toward the opponents goal line. The offense is allowed four downs to gain ten yards. If ten yards are gained within four downs, the offense is given four more downs to gain ten more yards. If they don't gain ten yards within four plays, the ball is turned over to the other team.

The team who does not have control of the football is on defense. The mission of the defensive unit is to defend its goal line and end zone by stopping the attack by the offensive team.

Tackling the ball carrier, causing and recovering fumbles, intercepting thrown passes and blocking kicked balls is what they do.

Two levels of personnel on offense are *blockers* and *skilled* positioned players. Blockers (called offensive linemen) are usually bigger and slower than skilled position players, and they do just one thing, block. On passing plays, these five players protect the thrower by retreating a few steps backwards while engaging the defense who's rushing the passer. On running plays, the offensive lineman charge forward to block the defensive line, allowing running backs to gain yards, thus advancing the ball towards the opponent's goal. Blockers are not allowed to catch a thrown forward pass. However, they can recover and advance fumbles and can catch and advance a forward pass tipped by a defender. But almost always blockers just block.

Skilled players on offense are those who run with the ball; catch the ball; throw the ball; and those who kick the ball. There are six skilled positioned players on offense.

The defensive unit consists of three levels; front *defensive linemen*, *linebackers* and *defense backs*.

The skilled position players are the linebackers and defensive backs.

BASIC OFFENSIVE POSITIONS

There are six basic skilled positions on offense.

There are quarterback (QB), halfback (HB), fullback (FB), tight end (TE), split end (SE) and flanker (or swingman) (FL).

There are three basic blocker positions. The offensive line positions are center (C), two guards (LG, RG) and two tackles (LT, RT). The center is set over the football at the line of scrimmage. Flanked to each side are the two guards. And the two tackles line up next to each guard. (See fig. 1-1)

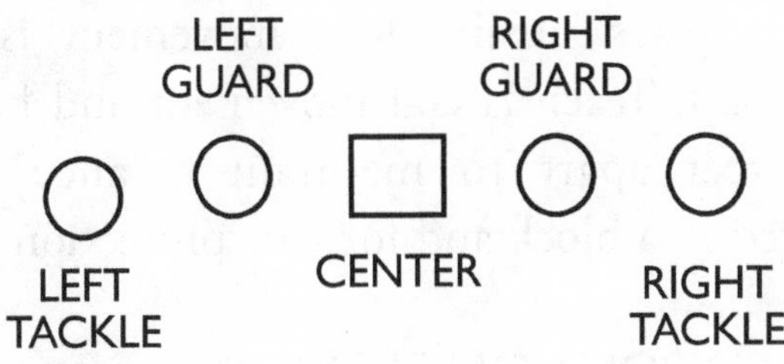

FIG. 1-1

OFFENSIVE LINE

At every position on the offensive line there is contact on every play. The *center* should be able to snap the ball between his legs quickly and effectively and block without hesitation. *Guards* are usually a bit faster and more agile. On sweeps and tosses (runs around the end) they must be able to quickly pull and move laterally down the line of scrimmage, turn up field and block.

Tackles are usually a bit bigger and strong enough to control any off-tackle play and must be quick on his feet to pass block, especially if he's protecting the quarterback's blind side.

It's important to teach your offensive line how to block.

The first step is very important when blocking head up or to slide in the gap. Teach how to cut off a pursuing linebacker and how to kick out block on the defensive end on a counter, sweep or toss plays. Again, foot movement is very important. Teach lateral movement and how to keep feet apart to maintain balance when engaged in a block and for pass protection.

SKILLED POSITION PLAYERS

The *quarterback* stands behind the center. The *running backs* are set behind the quarterback.

The *split end* and *flanker* (or slot man) usually line up wide from each tackle. And the *tight end* sets along side either tackle, depending on the formation. **(See fig. 1-2)**

Offensive sets can and do vary from play to play. An offensive set can have from zero to three

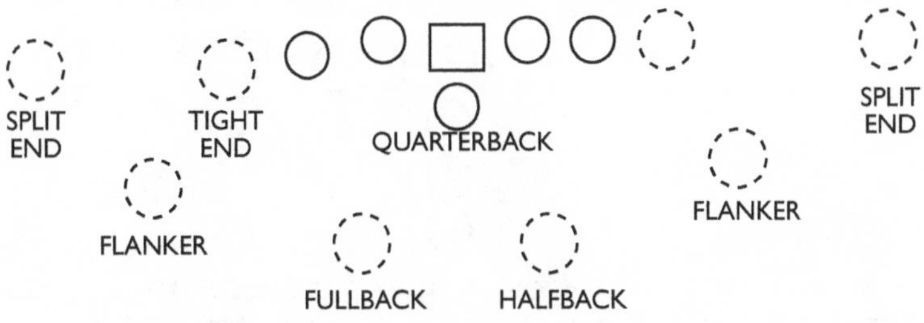

FIG. 1-2

running backs as well as from zero to five wide receivers. However, no matter what alignment an offense uses, **there must always be seven men on the line of scrimmage at the snap of the football.**

Neither offensive tackle can be at the end of the line. No matter what alignment you have in any formation, tackles must always be covered with skilled position players at both ends of the line of scrimmage. **(See fig. 1-3)**

Your *quarterback* is the most important player on the field. He calls the signals and initiates each play by receiving the ball (the snap) from the center. From there, on each play, the quarterback will either hand the ball off to a running back, throw the ball to any other skilled player, or he may run the football himself.

Wide receivers are the *split end* and *flanker* (running backs and tight ends may also line up as wide receivers). They line up wide of the tackles

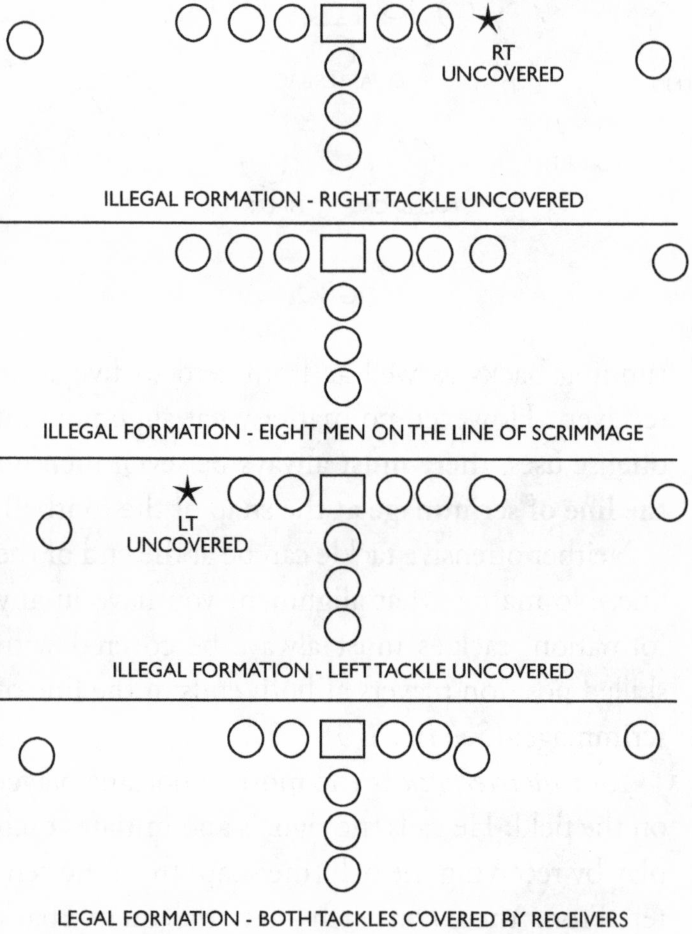

RT
UNCOVERED

ILLEGAL FORMATION - RIGHT TACKLE UNCOVERED

ILLEGAL FORMATION - EIGHT MEN ON THE LINE OF SCRIMMAGE

LT
UNCOVERED

ILLEGAL FORMATION - LEFT TACKLE UNCOVERED

LEGAL FORMATION - BOTH TACKLES COVERED BY RECEIVERS

FIG. 1-3

and tight end on the line of scrimmage. Your flanker should be the most agile skilled player and with the best field vision. The flanker has up to six positions to set in any formation before the snap of the football. (We'll get into more detail in Chapter 2) A good flanker has the ability to catch, run and throw the football with great competence.

Your *tight end* is most likely to be your most versatile skilled player. He must be able to block effectively, run precise pass routes and catch passes. He lines up next to either tackle on the line of scrimmage. He may be as big as an offensive tackle and be able to block defensive lineman and is light on his feet enough to find an open spot on the field, catch a pass and have the strength to shake off linebackers (LB) to gain extra yards.

Running backs, the halfbacks and fullbacks, are the most durable skilled players on the field.

They get hit and knocked down nearly every play and get back up for more. Backs must be able to block at the point of attack on running plays and pass block as well. And, of course, running backs run with the football. After securing the handoff, backs must hit the hole quickly and learn to read blocks on the go. Catching the ball is a plus for a running back. Being able to receive passes will help out your quarterback immensely and build his confidence as well. Practice passing to your running backs, screen passes and passes to the flats.

Basic Defensive Positions

On the field, the defense has three levels of attack. The *defensive lineman* (also called down linemen) consists of one or two defensive tackles (DT) and two defensive ends (DE). The *middle level* has two outside linebackers (OLB) and one or two inside linebackers (ILB). The last line of defense is *defensive backs*, two cornerbacks (CB) and one or two safeties (S). **(See fig, 1-4)**

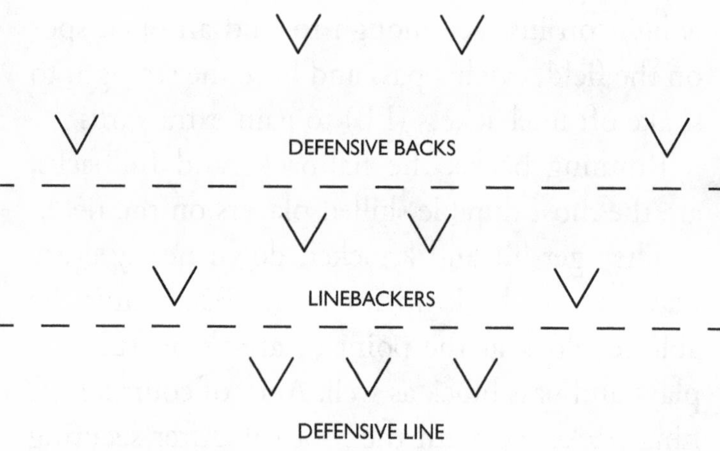

FIG. 1-4

Traditionally, at the line of scrimmage the defensive tackle(s) line up across from the center and guards. The defensive ends are anchored across the offensive tackles. The inside linebackers stand behind defensive line, at any spot from tackle to tackle. The outside linebackers are set 2-3 yards outside the DE's. The cornerbacks line up on both sides the line of scrimmage across from the SE and FL respectively. And finally, the safeties are in the middle of the field behind the linebackers with a view of all players on the field. (See fig. 1-5)

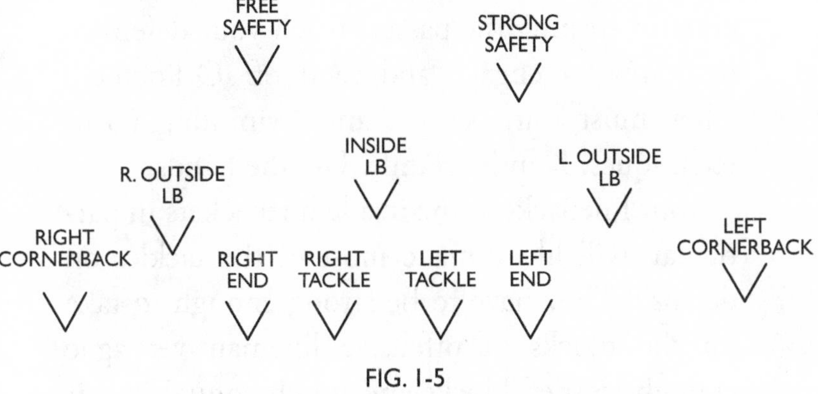

FIG. 1-5

Present day football defenses use a countless number of alignments. A 3-4 defense calls for three defensive linemen who are often lined up at various spots across the line of scrimmage, usually from offensive tackle to offensive tackle. In a 4-4 or 5-2 defense, the calls and assignments get even more complicated as we'll see in Chapter 5.

For defensive linemen, quickness will aid in

engaging blocks, shedding blocks and making tackles. Quickness will benefit them in slant and shooting the gap calls. D-linemen must also look out for trapping or pulling offensive linemen looking for the blind side block. Strength is a big asset in defeating the double team block. Also strength is necessary when occupying two offensive linemen to allow your linebackers to make tackles. And finally, D-linemen need to be efficient in rushing the passer. Teach your defensive line how to engage and fend off O-linemen. They must learn swerve and swimming (arm) techniques. Hands. Hands. Use the hands.

Your linebackers, the inside linebackers in particular, will likely make most of the tackles on defense. They have to be strong enough to take on the blocks of offensive lineman yet agile enough to shed blocks and tough enough to hit hard and make tackles. Teach your linebackers to shed the low cut block. Linebackers have to be dancers (sometimes even ballet dancers) to shed those low blocks at the feet and have the vision to keep their eyes on the football.

In today's football, even more is required from linebackers. LB's are the most versatile players on defense. At times, they must line up as down linemen at the line of scrimmage and help out with pass coverage, either dropping into zone coverage, picking up the running back out of the backfield, or in some cases, covering a wide receiver.

Having speed at the cornerback position will take a lot of pressure off your safeties. But not only speed, your CB's must be tough enough support the run on sweep or option plays and make big hits. Again, the cornerback must always force any and all outside running plays inside toward the center of the field where the pursuit help is.

In man-to-man pass coverage, the corner must peek inside and look in the quarterback's eyes. At the snap, he must read either run or pass immediately. If it's a pass, keep the receiver to the outside and stay on him. When playing 2 or 3 deep zones, the cornerback has a fraction more time to react to run or pass since he'll be positioned off the receiver a few yards in order to cover his zone quickly.

Your safeties are your last line of defense between your opponent and your goal line. They must be good tacklers and being big hitters is a plus. The free safety is usually the farthest from the line of scrimmage. In 2 deep zone coverage he covers the deep half of the field. In cover 3, the free safety covers the deep middle third of the field. In man-to-man pass coverage, the FS will line up on any open receiver. Supporting the run is vital for the FS. He must come up and make tackles up the middle, off-tackle and around the end. Quickness, good vision and having a nose for the football make a good free safety.

The strong safety has similar duties as the free safety; however, in some defensive calls he is free to move around to support the defense where it may be weak. The SS can position himself on the wide side of the field, drop into zone coverage, shadow the tight end, line up with the linebackers or help cover a receiver or double-team him.

No matter which alignment you use, your three levels of attack from the line of scrimmage remain the same. The beauty is that you can arrange and rearrange your defenses into countless alignments as we'll see in Chapter 5.

TWO

OFFENSIVE AND DEFENSIVE ALIGNMENTS

OFFENSIVE POSITIONING AND FORMATIONS

For every play from scrimmage in an entire game, the formation of the offensive line (also called interior linemen) stays the same. The center is over the ball flanked by two guards who have a tackle on their other side. **(See fig. 2-1)**

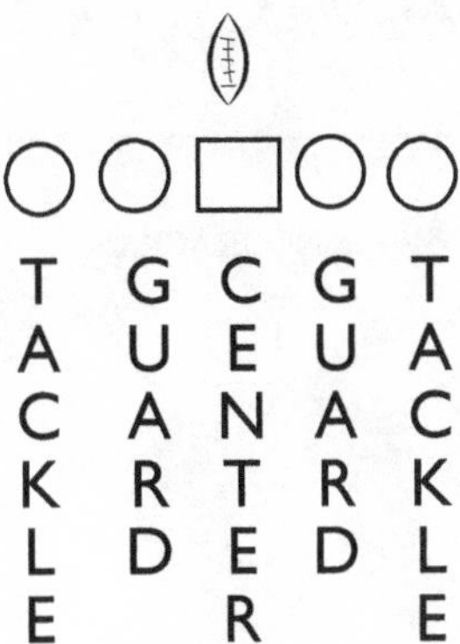

FIG. 2-1

The skilled position players can be aligned in an unlimited number of positions. Here's a list of basic formations for running backs: I, Power I, Pro, Pro Near or Far, T, Wishbone and Single back. (See fig. 2-2)

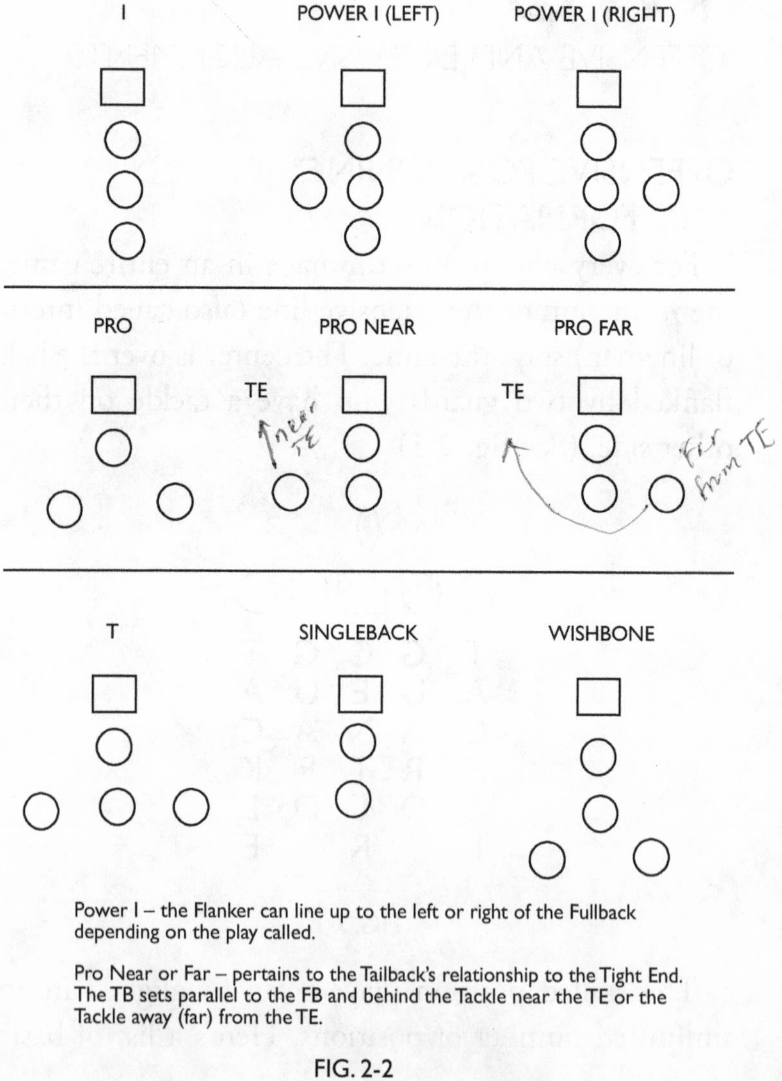

I

POWER I (LEFT)

POWER I (RIGHT)

PRO

PRO NEAR

TE

PRO FAR

TE

T

SINGLEBACK

WISHBONE

Power I – the Flanker can line up to the left or right of the Fullback depending on the play called.

Pro Near or Far – pertains to the Tailback's relationship to the Tight End. The TB sets parallel to the FB and behind the Tackle near the TE or the Tackle away (far) from the TE.

FIG. 2-2

Note: Near and Far pertain to the tailback in relationship to the tight end. The TB is either set behind the tackle NEAR the tight end or set behind the tackle FAR from the TE.

LINE FORMATIONS

The tight end lines up next to either tackle. He can split 3-5 yards from the tackle. This is called "flex". The TE can also be split wide of the offensive linemen as long as he stays on the line of scrimmage. Some plays call for the split end and flanker to be on the line of scrimmage. In those cases, the TE will line up a yard or two off the line.

Just like running backs, the split end, flanker and tight end have many alignments at their deposal. The TE is always on either the left or right side of the interior linemen, tight, flex or split. (See fig. 2-3)

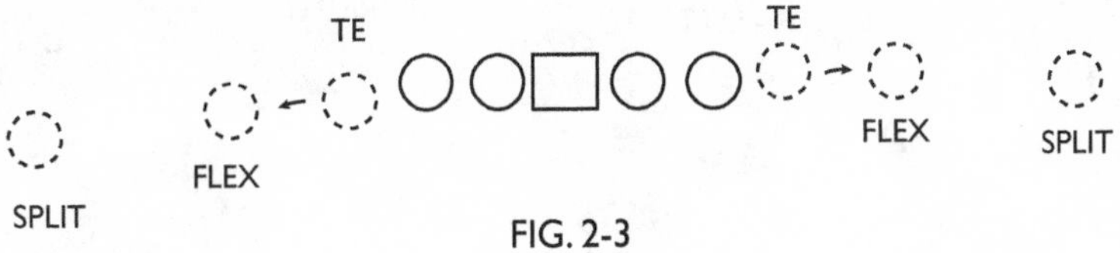

TE TE

FLEX FLEX

SPLIT SPLIT

FIG. 2-3

The split end is always lined up on the left or right side of the line, opposite of the TE, wide, flex or tight. (**See fig. 2-4**)

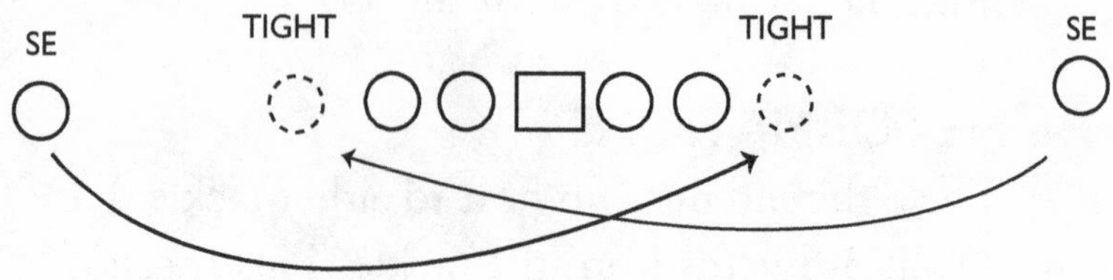

FIG. 2-4

As a receiver, the flanker has five basic positions. The "A" position is the slot between the tackle and SE on either side. "L" is the wide position opposite of the split end. "F" (or Flip) is on the outside of the SE. And "R" is the wing-left or wing-right 2-yards by 2-yards position outside of the tackle or TE. (**See fig. 2-5a**)

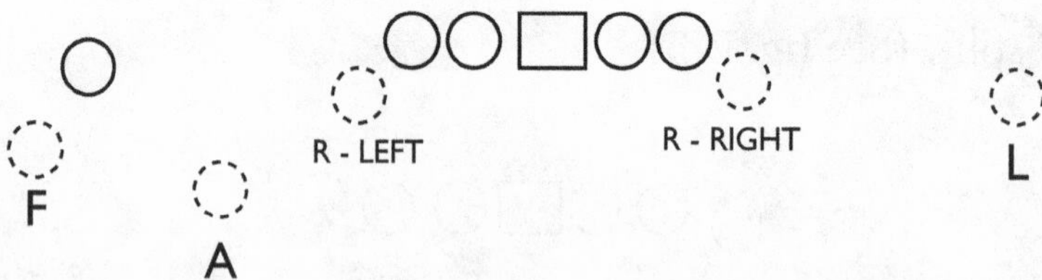

FIG. 2-5A

As a runner, the FL can line up in the "Power Left" or "Power Right" positions. Or he can be in the "T" or "Wishbone" formations. **(See fig. 2-5b)**

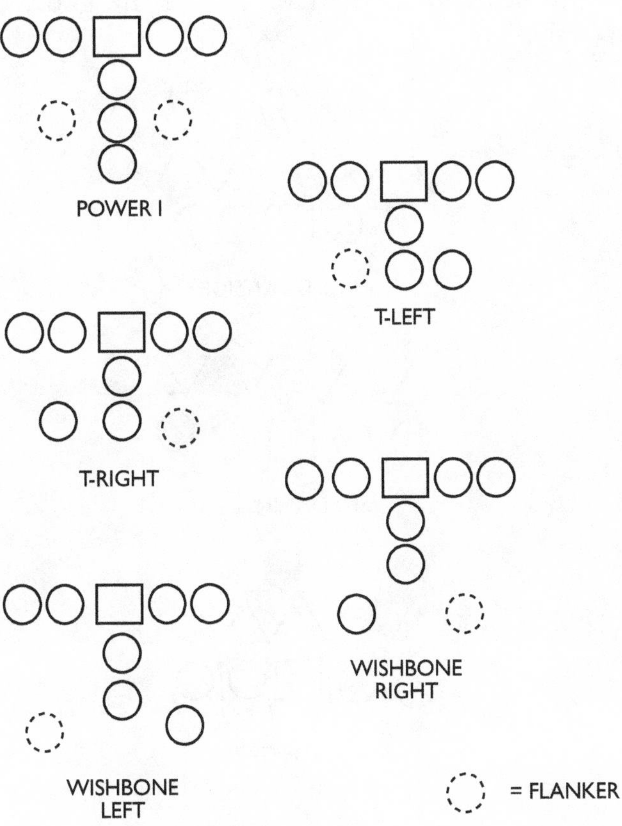

FIG. 2-5B

DEFENSIVE POSITIONING AND FORMATIONS

The defensive linemen (also called the defensive front) play on the line of scrimmage directly across from the offensive linemen. According to the defensive play called, the defensive front can align "head up", "shaded" or "in the gap". (See fig. 2-6)

FIG. 2-6

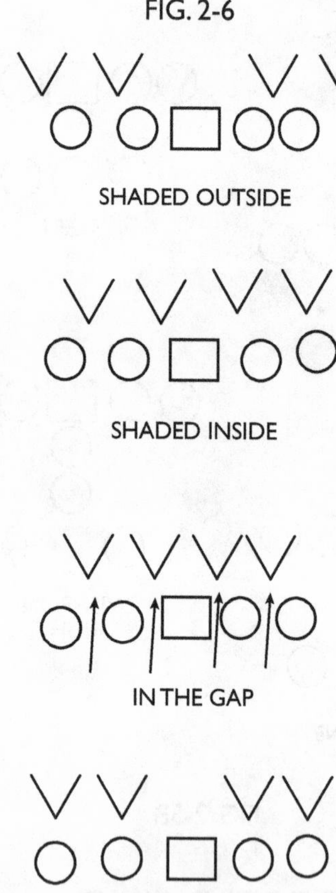

SHADED - NOT TOTALLY IN THE GAP BUT LINED UP ON THE OFFENSIVE LINEMAN'S SHOULDER.

Linebackers have wide latitude of positions in which to set. Usually, in a 4-man front, the inside linebacker will set somewhere between both offensive guards. The two outside linebackers will line up on the outside shoulder of any tight ends or about two yards outside the offensive tackle. In a 3-man front, the two inside linebackers will line up on the outside shoulders of both guards or between guard and tackle. The two OLB will set similar to a 4-man front. (**See fig.** 2-7)

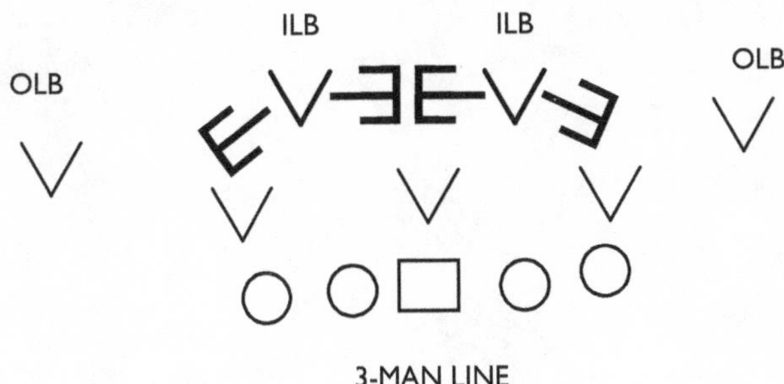

3-MAN LINE

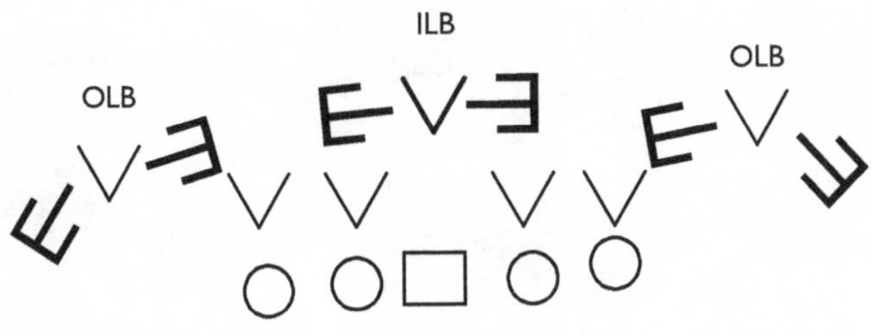

4-MAN LINE

FIG. 2-7

Cornerbacks line up according to what defense is called and/or what alignment the offense presents. If in man-to-man coverage, the CB will line up wherever the wide receivers line up. It could be on the same side of the field or on opposite sides. And accordingly, the safeties will match up with their assigned player. When playing a zone, the CB and safeties set up in their respective positions. And at the snap of the ball cover their assigned areas. **(See fig. 2-8)**

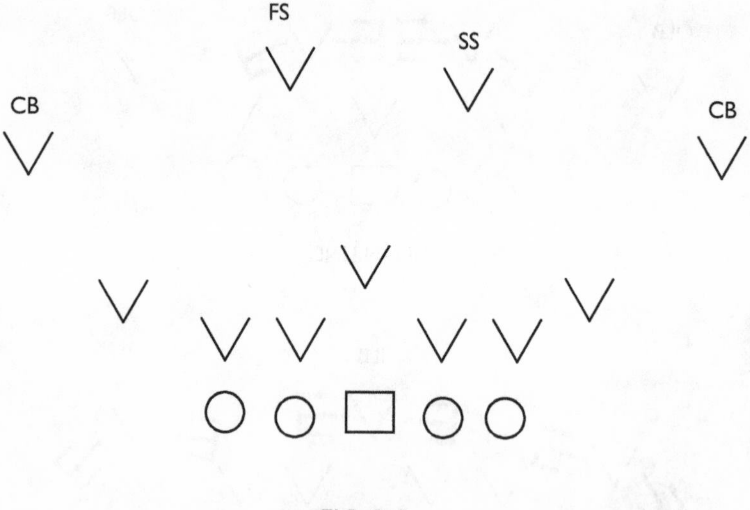

FIG. 2-8

THREE

PLAY NAMES AND HOLE NUMBERING

The naming of running plays is simply a combination of who's carrying the football and where they are going. Hole numbering helps to achieve this. For running plays, the traditional "left-side odd/right-side even" system of whole numbering is still used by many high schools and recreational football leagues across the country. It's a good and easy system to remember. The spaces between offensive linemen to the left of the center are numbered 1, 3, 5, and 7. On the right side on center they are numbered 2, 4, 6, and 8. (See fig. 3-1)

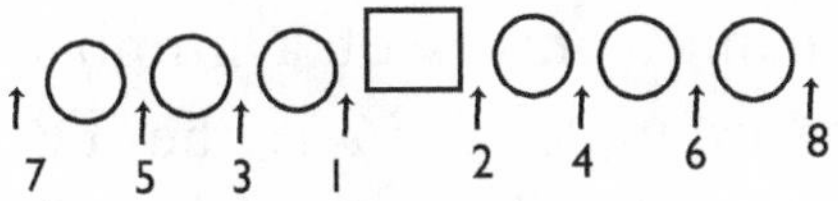

7 5 3 1 2 4 6 8

FIG. 3-1

Now that we have holes, we need players to run through them. Offensive skilled positions are designated by numbers to facilitate our objective. Quarterback (QB)-1, Fullback (FB)-2, Halfback (HB)-3, Flanker (FL)-4, (FL-8 for pass plays) Tight End (TE)-7 and Split End (SE)-9. **(See fig. 3-2)**

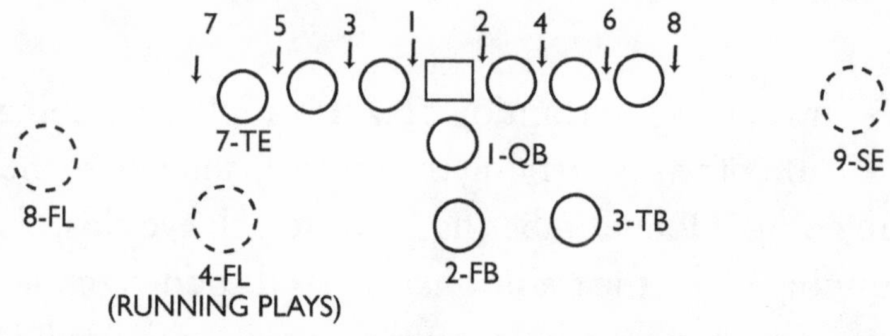

FIG. 3-2

Examples: If the fullback carries the ball through the 4-hole, the play would be called "24". If the tailback carries the ball through the 5-hole, the play would be called "35". A sweep, toss, option or reverse are plays that go around either end of the line. It ends in either "7" or "8", as in a "47 reverse" or a "38 toss sweep".

A play name consists of a number and the action. For example, a 34 is the TB running through the 4 hole. The action is how the TB will run through the hole. Give, Dive, Veer, Blast, Counter, Draw, Isolation, Kick out, Off-tackle, Sweep, Slot Inside, Sweep, Sneak, Option and Bootleg are the actions of running plays.

PLAY DEFINITIONS

Give or Dive – A simple handoff straight ahead.

Veer – A quick-hitting handoff where QB rides the handoff to the back and the routes are determined by the slant of the defensive linemen. If a hole is there the handoff is made. If the defense collapses on the runner, the QB keeps the ball and runs around the end.

Blast – A quick-hitting handoff through the 1, 2, 3 or 4 holes.

Counter – A fake handoff or motion in one direction then a give to the back in the opposite direction against the pursuit of the defense.

Draw – The QB drops back like he's going to throw a pass, but instead turns and hands the ball to a running back.

Isolation – A double-team block up front which isolates the linebacker who is blocked by the fullback. It's usually run through the 3, 4, 5, or 6 holes.

**Off-tackle – A running play through the 5 or 6 holes.

**Kick out – A running play through the 5 or 6 holes with the FB blocking (kicking out) the defensive end.

**Reverse – A handoff to a running back and runs laterally behind the line of scrimmage then hands it off to a receiver running in the opposite direction.

**Sweep – A running play around the 7 and 8 holes.

**Pitch or Toss – The act of the QB tossing the ball to a running back that is moving laterally away from him.

**Option – A run around the end by the QB with the option to pitch it backwards (at the threat of being tackled) or throw the football.

**Bootleg – A run around the opposite end by the QB after faking a hand-off the other direction.

**Rollout – A lateral sprint by the QB to either side of the field with the intent of throwing the football.

**Screen – A forward pass thrown to a running back or wide receiver behind the line of scrimmage, just out of the reach of an on charging defense, with blockers in front of him.

PLAY CALLING

When calling running plays you are doing more than just saying who gets the ball and where it's going. Play calling tells everybody where they should be aligned at the snap of the ball. A play call identifies all skilled position players and where they should be aligned when the ball is snapped. The first segment of the call is the backfield formation (I, Pro, T, Near, Far, Wishbone, Power I). Next segment, where is the tight end is aligned (left, right, flex, split). Then the flanker positions (A, R, L, F, Power wing left or right). Next is any motion. Finally, the play number (the ball carrier through a particular whole).

The method is the same for both running and passing plays. First is the backfield formation. Second is the tight end position. Third is the flanker position. Fourth is any motion. Fifth is the play number or pass routes. For example, if you call "I, Right,A,34 Isolation" it would look like this:

*The running backs are in the "I" formation.

*The TE is on the right side of the line.

*The FL is in the "A" position.

*The ball is given to the TB (#3-man) and he runs through the 4-hole.

The play "pro, left, L, 21 dive" is simply with the running backs in the pro (or split back) formation, the TE lined up next to the LT, the FL is wide out on the TE side and the ball is given to the FB (#2-man) and he runs through the 1-hole:

*The running backs are in the "Pro" formation.

*The TE is on the left side of the line.

*The FL is in the "L" position.

*The ball is given to the FB (#2-man) and he runs through the 1-hole.

—Here is a list of basic names of running plays.

FULLBACK:

21 & 22 Give, Dive
23 & 24 Dive
25 & 26 Veer or Give

TAILBACK:

31 & 32 Blast, Counter or Draw
33 & 34 Isolation or Counter
35 & 36 Kick Out or Off-tackle
37 & 38 Sweep

FLANKER:

41 & 42 Slot Inside, Dive
43 & 44 Counter
45 & 46 Off-tackle
47 & 48 Slot Reverse or Sweep

QUARTERBACK:

11 & 12 QB Sneak
17 & 18 Option or Bootleg
17 & 18 QB Sweep

PASS PLAYS

Passing plays are called according to the "passing tree". *Odd numbers* (except 9) are pass routes go towards the sidelines. *Even numbers* are pass routes go toward the middle of the field. (**See fig. 3-3**).

Pass plays can get confusing to youngsters. So, remember to make it simple. However, your quarterback has to understand the basics of the passing tree (if he can't grasp the basics of this tree, create a pass system that all your quarterbacks will understand). Your SE, TE and FL are designated as numbers 9, 7, and 8 respectively. They can also be referred to as x, y and z.

Calling a pass play begins with the same sequence as a running play. There's the formation of the running backs, the TE positioning, the FL alignment and then your pass routes. There are three (3) ways that your quarterback can call pass routes in the huddle. First, there is the xyz system, which may be the easiest. When calling the route the QB simply says the position then the route. For example: X-9, Y-4, and Z-8, meaning SE runs a fly pattern, TE runs a drag (or in, crossing) route and the FL runs a post. Another way to call route in the xyz pattern is to just call out

PASSING TREE

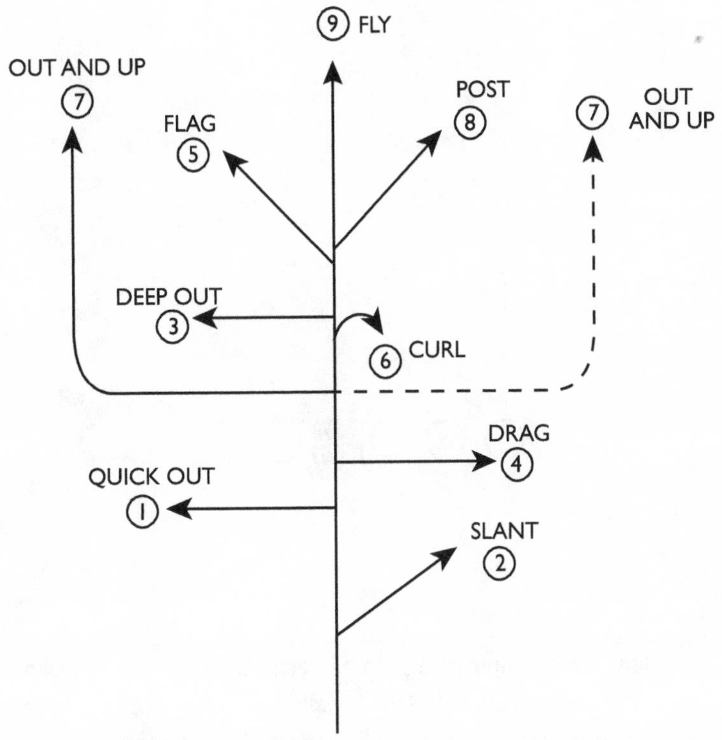

* ODD NUMBERED ROUTES GO TOWARDS THE SIDELINES.

* EVEN NUMBERED ROUTES GO TOWARDS THE MIDDLE OF THE FIELD.

* THE 7 ROUTE CAN BE RUN FROM EITHER SIDE OF THE FIELD.

FIG. 3-3

the numbers, 9-4-8. Each receiver will know what their route pattern is no matter how they are aligned at the line of scrimmage. (See fig. 3-4a)

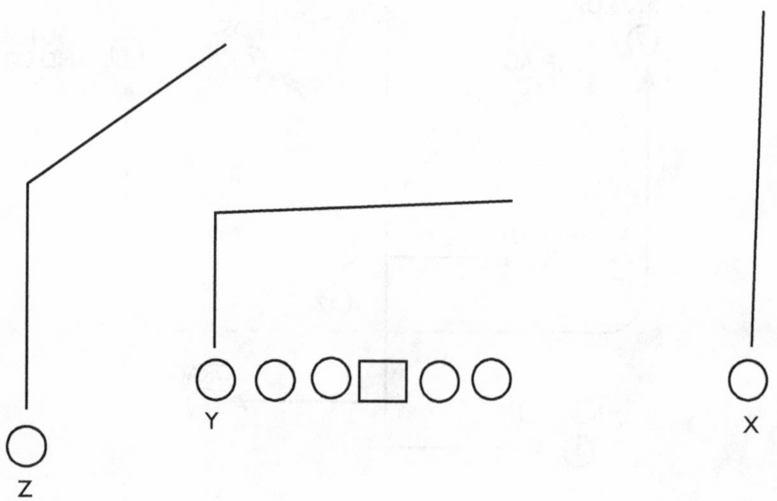

In this example, the pass patterns are called in xyz order. Pass play "Left, L, 9-4-8" is called. The 9 route is for the SE. The 4 route is for the TE. And the FL runs the 8 route.

FIG. 3-4A

A more advanced way to call routes is how the receivers are aligned at the snap of the ball from left to right. For example: if you call "I, Left, A, 8-9-4", your TE is the first receiver from left to right so he going to run a POST pattern. The FL is next in line. He'll run a FLY route. And the SE is last, running a drag across the middle. **(See fig. 3-4b)**

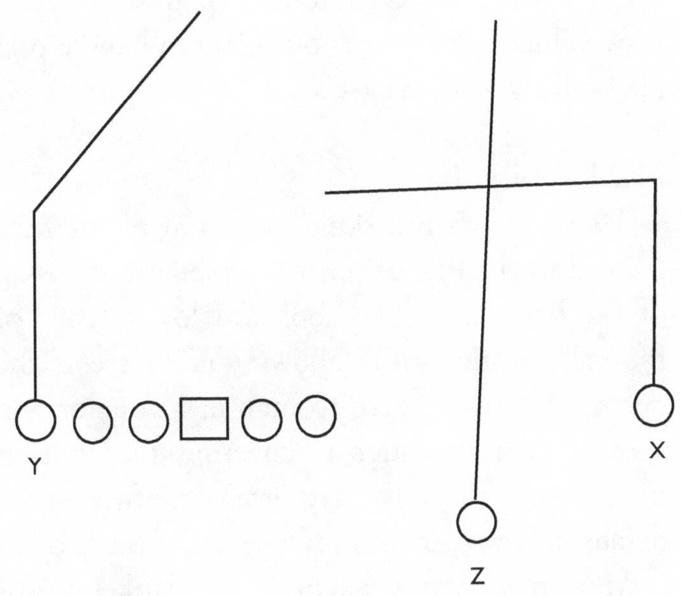

In this example, pass play "Left, A, 8-9-4 is called.
The routes are determined by where the receivers are aligned at snap.
The TE runs an 8 route. The FL runs a 9 route. And the SE runs a 4 route.

FIG. 3-4B

One more way to make calling pass plays simpler for your quarterback is to have him refer to his receivers as 70, 80 and 90. Then just tell each number (receiver) what pattern to run. For example, "70 in – 80 post – 90 fly". (**See fig. 3-5a**) Or he can call "80 in – 70 fly – 90 slant". (**See fig. 3-5b**) There is no certain order in which your QB has to call the routes. Keep it simple and easy. Whichever system your QB can handle pass play calling, do it that way.

MOTION

Motion is when a skilled position player runs parallel to the line of scrimmage before the snap of the ball. In high school and lower levels of football, motion only allows you to see if the defense is playing man-to-man or a zone or will show which defender is covering the motion man. Your motion may even confuse some defenses. Don't let your offense be confused by it.

Motion is simply having your flanker (most often), TE, or running backs motion into the proper alignment before the ball is snapped. Motion is determined as in relation to the football. There are three (3) designated motion directions: Over, In and Away (OIA). "**Over**" motion is motion over the ball, the motion man running laterally past the center. "**In**" motion is the running in towards the ball but doesn't cross the center before the snap. And "**Away**" motion is the

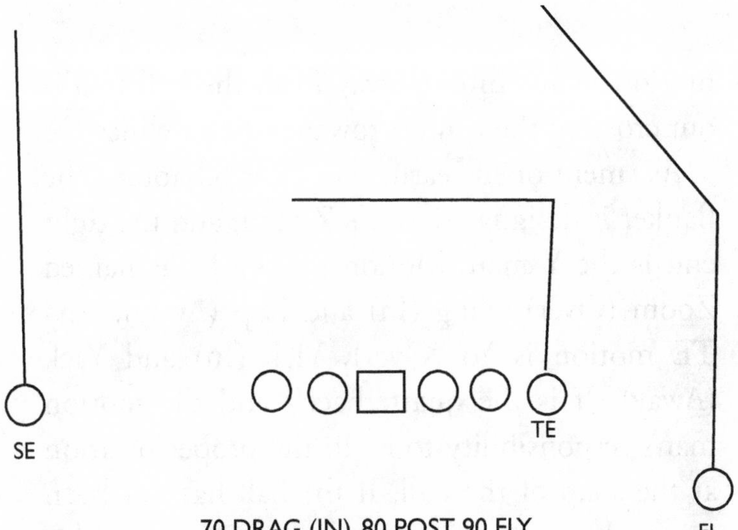

SE

TE

FL

70 DRAG (IN), 80 POST, 90 FLY

FIG. 3-5A

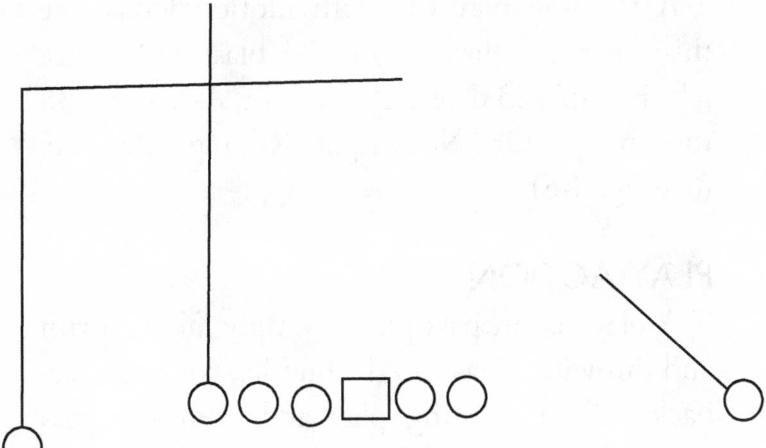

80 IN, 70 FLY, 90 SLANT

FIG. 3-5B

motion man running away from the ball (without crossing the center) towards the sidelines.

As mentioned earlier in this chapter, the flanker is designated as the Z man, and the tight end is the Y man. Motion for the FL is named Zoom (Over), Zing (In) and Zap (Away). Any TE motion is Yo (Over), Yick (In) and Yack (Away). It is the quarterback's and the motion man's responsibility to be in the proper position at the snap of the ball. If the ball has not been snapped by the time the motion man reaches his designated spot, he should stop and set or jog in place until the snap.

A running play call with motion looks like this: "Far, left-flex, L-"yo", 34 blast". Or "Pro, left, F-"zap", 23 dive". Or "I, right, A-"zoom", 38 toss sweep". Or "Near, right, R-"zing", 22 dive. **(See fig. 3-6)**

PLAY ACTION

A play action pass play is simply faking a run and throwing a pass. In the huddle, your quarterback calls a running play and then the pass routes. For example: "Pro, left, A, 34 Isolation, 4-9-6. This is a fake to the tailback running the 34 Isolation and a pass to the In, Fly or Curl routes. (x-y-z) Or: "Near, right, L-"zoom", 22 Give,

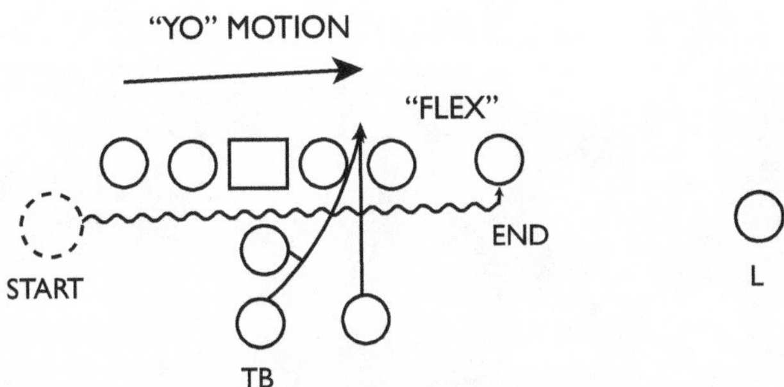

NEAR, RIGHT - FLEX - "YO", L, 34 ISOLATION

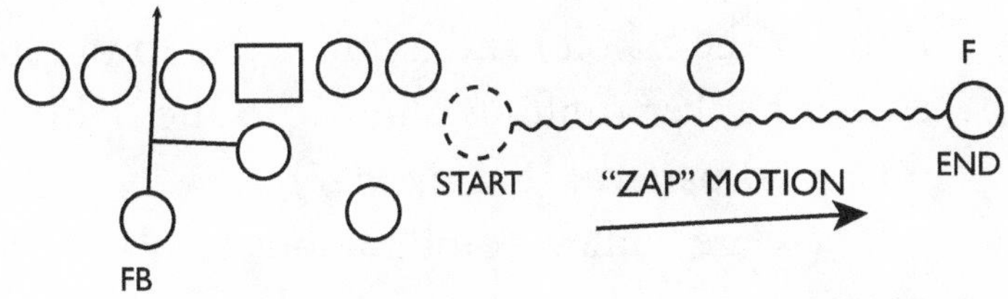

PRO, LEFT, F - "ZAP", 23 DIVE

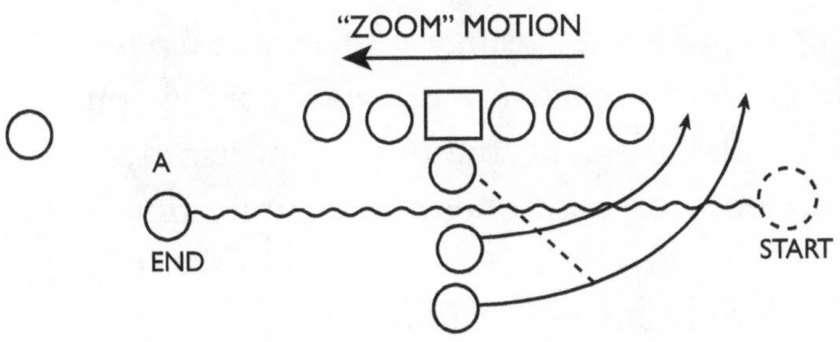

I, RIGHT, A – "ZOOM," 38 TOSS SWEEP

FIG. 3-6

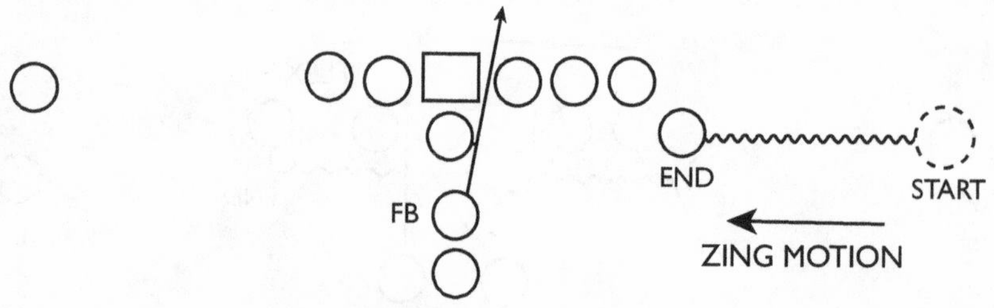

I, RIGHT, WING RIGHT, "ZING," 22 DIVE

FIG. 3-6

1-6-1". This is fake to the fullback (the 2 man through the 2 hole) and a quick pass to the split end or flanker running Outs or to the tight end on a Curl pattern. **(See fig. 3-7)**

There are endless combinations of play action passes. Use them accordingly and wisely. Remember, play action passes work well only if you've been running the football effectively. Faking the run and passing is just a waste of energy when your opponent has been stopping your running plays all game, but more importantly, it's a waste of precious seconds of pass protection.

BACKFIELD MOVEMENT AND SHIFTING

Shifting and movement in the backfield before the snap is designed to get a read on the defense's alignment. Shifting is simply the skilled offensive

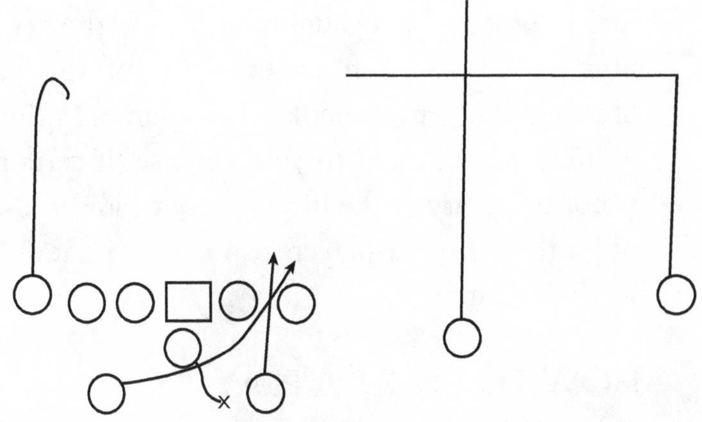

PRO, LEFT, A, 34 ISOLATION, 4-9-6
(—RUN—) (—PASS—)

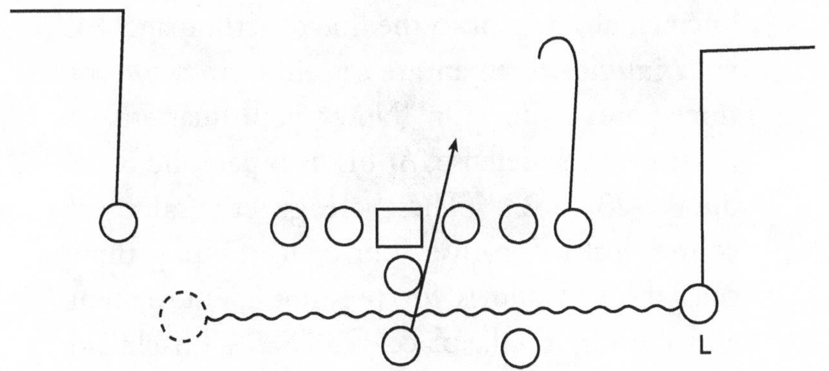

NEAR, RIGHT, L - "ZOOM", 22 GIVE, 1-6-1

PLAY ACTION PASSES

FIG. 3-7

players freely moving from position to position into their called play alignment before the beginning of any motion or the snap of the ball. Shifting and movement is just an additional wrinkle you can add to your offense. It certainly is not necessary at the high school or lower levels of football. If your players can master it, and if it works, use it.

HOW TO START A PLAY

Each coach has his own system of how he wants to start a play. Here's a standard call to get the ball snapped. From the huddle, the offensive linemen always trot to the line of scrimmage. All your interior linemen are set either in a two or three point stance. On "Now", your quarterback looks over the defense. At his own pace, he barks out "2-23, 2-23. (These are generic calls. Of course, feel free to use your own). During these calls the QB allows for pre-motion movement and shifting to take place. On "Set" all backfield movement should be finished. Then the final motion (if any) begins. The generic snap count is always on "two". Your QB barks "Go, Go" (or hut, hut) and the ball is snapped. Again, your QB is in control. The ball is snapped when "he" is ready.

Here's a sequence of starting a play:

** "Now" – Your quarterback stands tall with authority behind center and looks over the defense.

** "2-23", "2-23" – During these signal calls, your QB allows for all shifting and movement to take place.

** "Set" – On set all backfield movement and shifting is finished or is finished within seconds. (When the QB is ready, a head bob or foot nod starts motion, if any).

** "Go", "Go" - On the second "go" (or whatever your snap count) the motion man should be at his appropriate position as the ball is snapped. Again, your quarterback is in control.

FOUR

OFFENSIVE LINE BLOCKING SCHEMES

There's always the tendency to make this part of the game very complicated. Don't. For high school, junior high, recreational, rocket and pee wee football leagues, blocking schemes must be simple but effective. The play in the trenches is the essence of football. Offensive line blocking is probably the most important dimension of football and yet can be very basic. It's man on man, hand to hand combat for 5-8 seconds every 40 seconds. Every play from scrimmage starts with blocking up front.

Each offensive lineman has only three (3) different reads with respect to the defensive line. These are: *Head-up.* That's when a defensive lineman is lined up directly in front of an offensive lineman. *Gap.* That's when the defense is lined up in the gaps across from the offensive line. And *Uncovered.* That's when there is no one in front or in the gap of the offensive linemen. **(See fig. 4-1)**

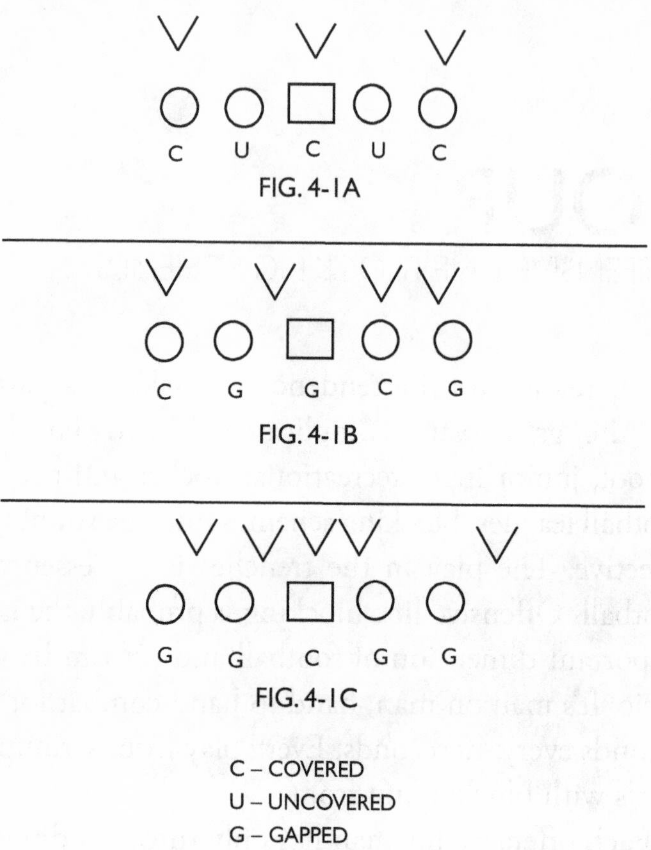

In ***Fig. 4-1a,*** *the offensive line blocking assignments are quite basic. The center and both tackles have opponents lined head up on them.* ***In Fig.4-1b*** *only the LT and the RG are covered. The LG, C and RT have gap responsibilities, depending on the play called.* ***In Fig. 4-1c,*** *only the center is covered, and the other linemen have gap responsibilities.*

There are two types of blocking for offensive

linemen, onside and offside blocking. Onside blocking is simply the blocking schemes on the side of the center that the play is run. For instance, if you run a 34 isolation then the C, RG and RT have "onside" blocking assignments. The offside blocking is left of the center. Conversely, if a 35 isolation was called, the C, LG and LT will block onside and the blocks to the right of the center are offside blocks. (Note: The center blocks every play as an onside blocking assignment, either to the left or the right.) **(See fig.4-2a)**

In fig. 4-2b*, the right guard and right tackle have onside blocking assignments. If head up, gapped or shaded the linemen attack and drive, turning their butts to the right. If either lineman is totally uncovered, he blocks down to a double team block. On double team blocks, the onside guard helps the center and the tackle helps the guard. On 1 or 2 hole plays, the guard will always double team block if gapped or shaded.*

The offside guard and tackle with head up or gapped responsibilities will attack and drive towards the play hole. If totally uncovered, they will attack the first linebacker or safety in sight going towards the side of the play. **(See fig. 4-2c)**

NOTE: On plays to the 7 or 8 holes, the onside guard will pull down the line and block through the hole.

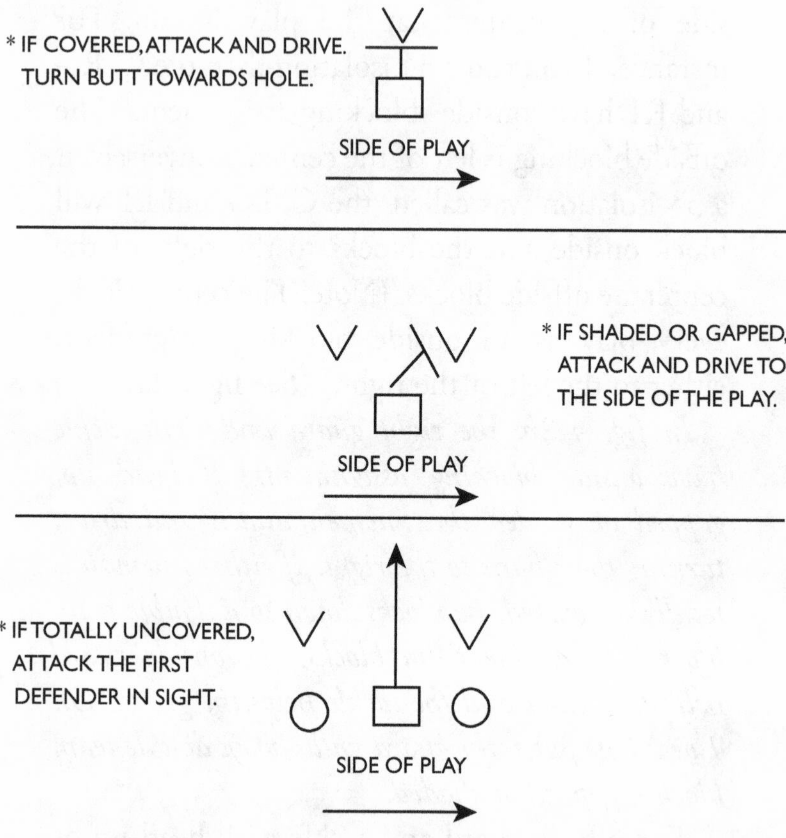

ONSIDE AND OFFSIDE BLOCKING FOR THE CENTER IS THE SAME.

FIG. 4-2A

ONSIDE BLOCKING

* IF GAPPED, GUARD AND TACKLE ATTACKS AT HOLE AND DRIVES OPPOSITE OF PLAY

* GUARD DRIVES AHEAD. TACKLE BLOCKS DOWN

* IF COVERED, ATTACK AND DRIVE TURNING BUTT TOWARDS THE HOLE

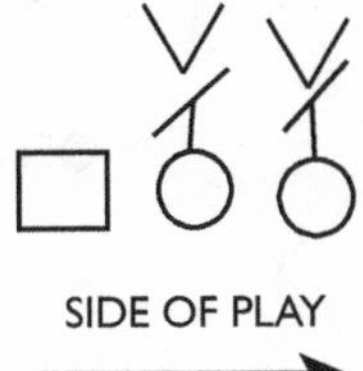

ON PLAYS TO THE 7 AND 8 HOLES, OFFISDE AND ONSIDE GUARDS AND/OR TACKLES MAY PULL AROUND INTO HOLES TO LEAD BLOCK, IF DESIRED.

FIG. 4-2B

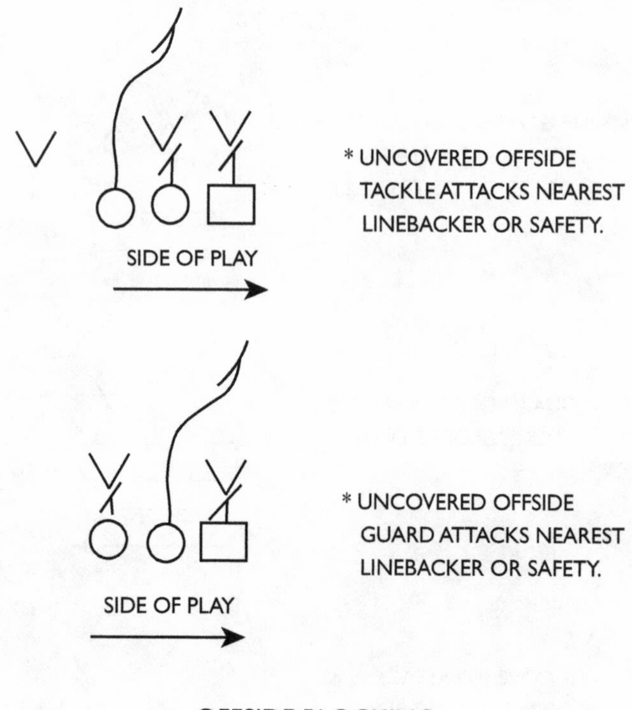

OFFSIDE BLOCKING

FIG. 4-2c

FIVE

BASIC DEFENSES

Again, as with respect to defensive schemes, play calls and audibles on the high school, junior high, pee wee and recreational league level, simplicity is the key. Keep it simple. There are five (5) basic defenses that should be sufficient enough to be competitive and successful. These are called the 3-4, 4-4, 4-3, 5-2 and 6-1 defenses. The first digit is the number of down linemen, and the second digit represents the number of linebackers for that set. **(See fig. 5-1)**

The 4-3, 4-4, 5-2 and 6-1 are excellent defenses against the run. The 3-4, 4-3 and 4-4 defenses give you the flexibility in defending the run or pass. All five defenses are excellent for *slants* and *shooting the gaps* calls. However, the 4-3 and 4-4 are best for the *engage and read* defensive call.

The general idea of every defense is to collapse or rally to the football. The job of defensive ends, outside linebackers and cornerbacks is to contain and force every running play towards the middle of the field where the defensive pursuit help is waiting.

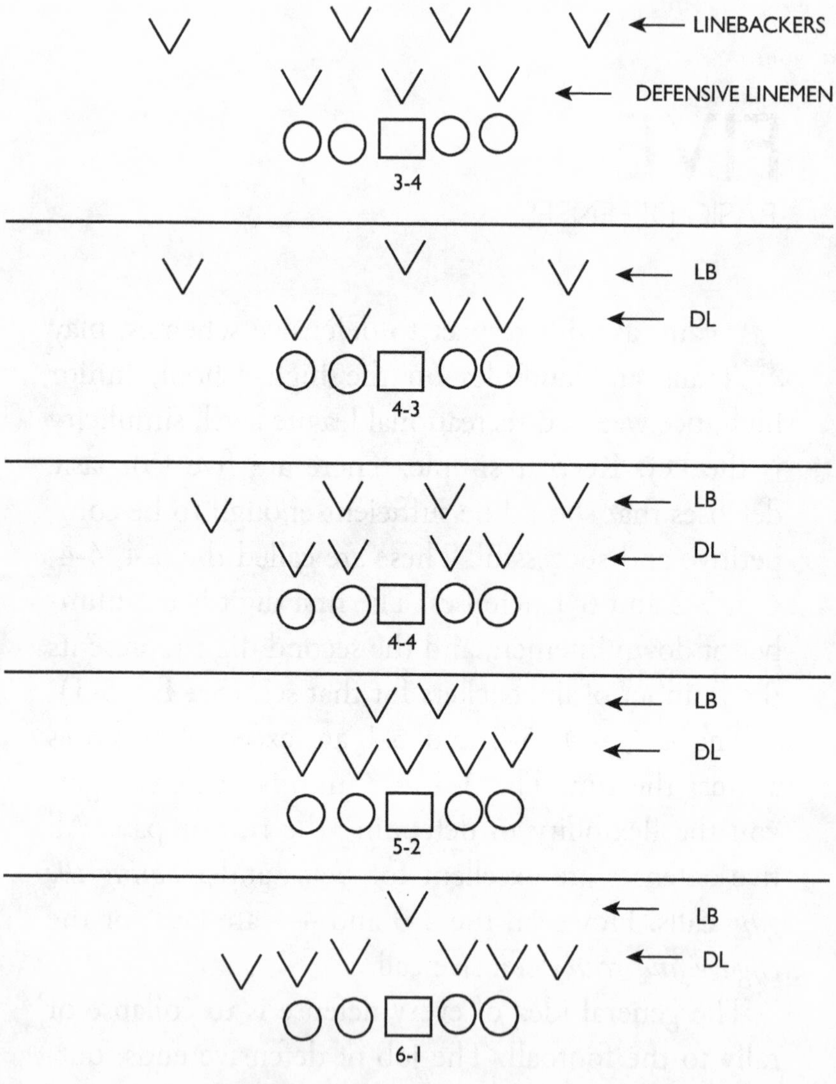
LINEBACKERS
DEFENSIVE LINEMEN
3-4
LB
DL
4-3
LB
DL
4-4
LB
DL
5-2
LB
DL
6-1

FIG. 5-1

DEFENSIVE LINEMEN

The defensive line has three (3) assignments: SLANT, SHOOT and ENGAGE & READ. **Slant** is when the defensive linemen are head-up on the offensive linemen, and at the snap he slants to the hole to the left or right. **(See. Fig. 5-2a)** **Shoot** is when the D-linemen line up in the gap and shoot through at the snap. **(See fig. 5-2b)** The **engage and read** technique is used most with stronger players on high school varsity teams. Just as the name implies, at the snap the defensive linemen engage their opponents, reads the play and flows to the ball carrier and hopefully shedding the block to make the tackle. **(See fig. 5-2c)**

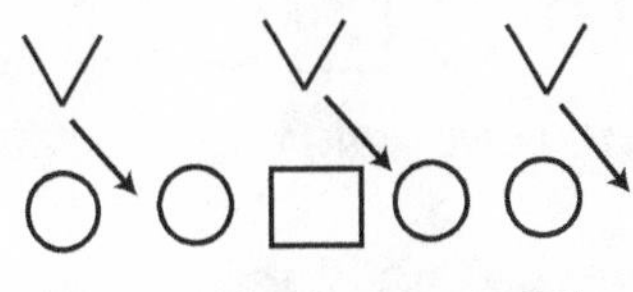

3 – MAN LINE – SLANT LEFT

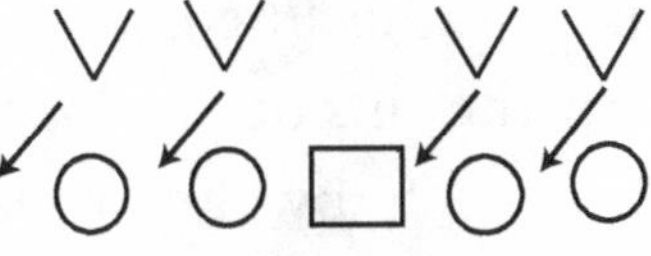

4 – MAN LINE – SLANT RIGHT

* ON MOST SLANT CALLS, THE DEFENSIVE LINEMEN ARE LINED HEAD UP ON THE OFFENSIVE LINEMEN AND SLANTS IN THE CALLED DIRECTION.

FIG. 5-2A

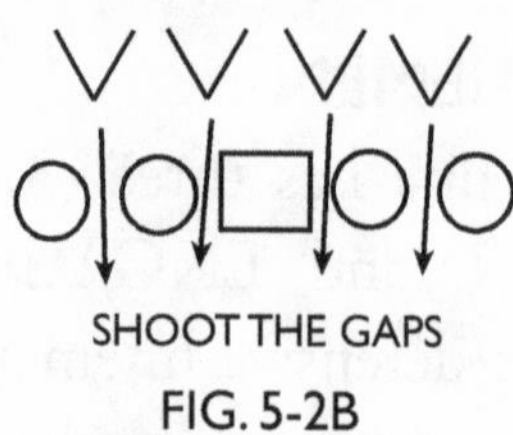

SHOOT THE GAPS

FIG. 5-2B

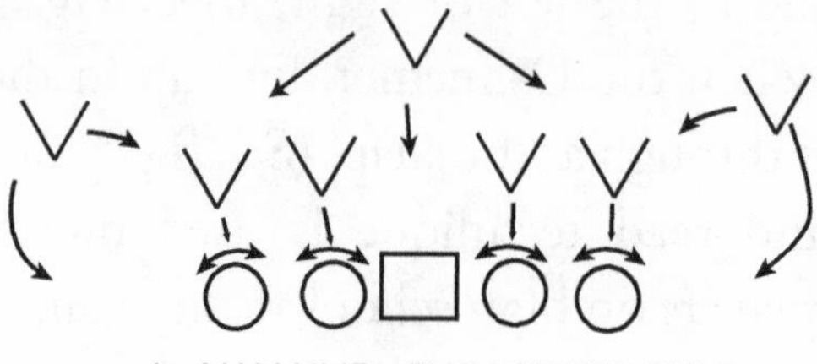

4 – MAN LINE – ENGAGE AND READ

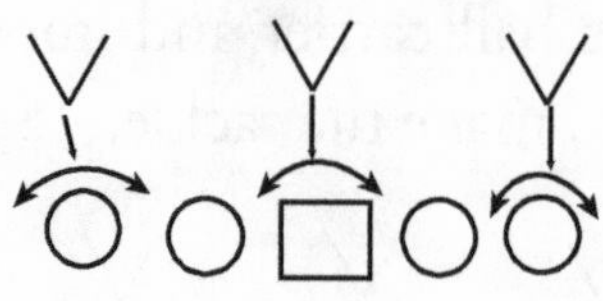

3 – MAN LINE – ENGAGE AND READ

FIG. 5-2C

Inside linebackers fill the holes on running plays according to the linemen's defensive call. On SLANTS, the inside linebackers fill the unoccupied holes left by the slanting linemen. The three D-linemen are head-up on the center and two tackles. If they slant to the left, the left ILB fills the guard/tackle hole and the right ILB fills the center/guard hole on their respective sides. If the SLANT is right, then the reverse is true. The left inside linebacker fills the center/guard hole and the right ILB plugs the guard/tackle hole. (**See fig. 5-3**)

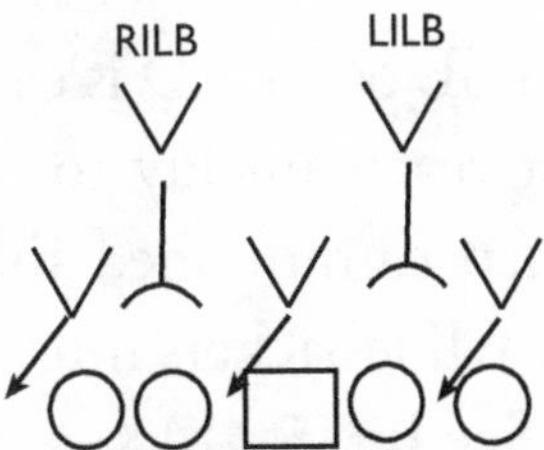

* 3 – MAN LINE – SLANT RIGHT – THE LEFT ILB FILLS THE CENTER/GUARD HOLE. THE RIGHT ILB FILLS THE GUARD/TACKLE HOLE.

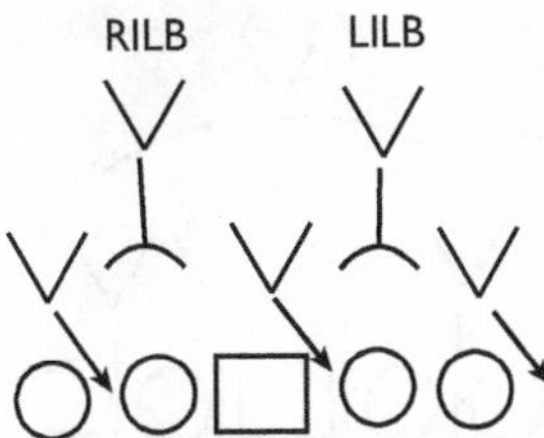

* 3 – MAN LINE – SLANT LEFT – THE LEFT ILB FILLS THE GUARD/TACKLE HOLE. THE RIGHT ILB FILLS THE CENTER/GUARD HOLE.

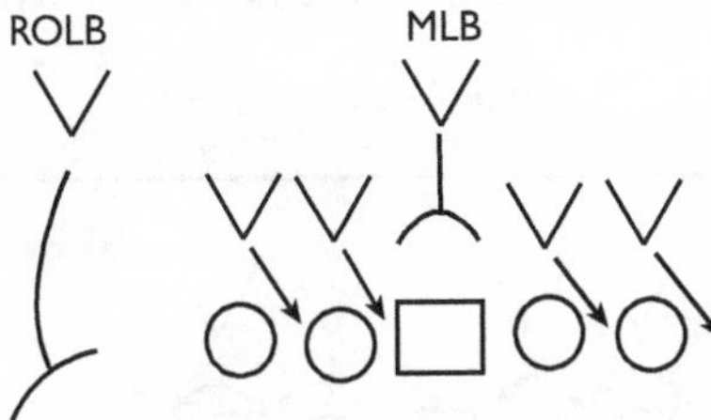

* 4 – MAN LINE – SLANT LEFT – THE MIDDLE LB FILLS THE CENTER/GUARD HOLE. THE RIGHT OLB MUST COVER THE RIGHT END OF THE LINE OF SCRIMMAGE.

FIG. 5-3

Since all the interior holes will be plugged by the defensive front on a SHOOT call, the ILB is free to rove to either side to make a play. (**See fig. 5-4a**)

When ENGAGE & READ is called, the inside linebacker must react quickly to the football. If the front linemen cannot shed their blocks fast enough then ALL linebackers must be in position for the tackle. (**See fig. 5-4b**)

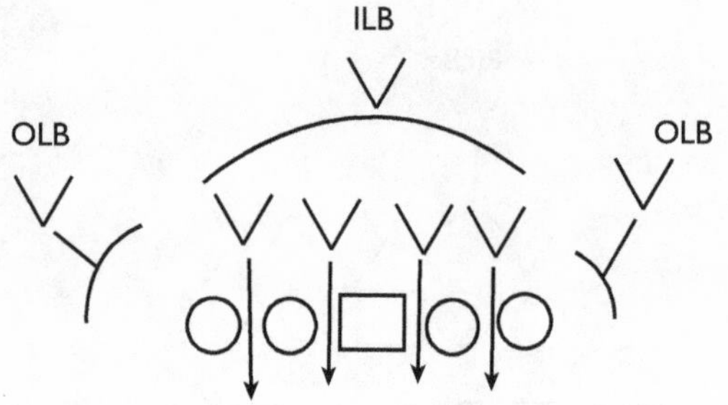

ILB

OLB

OLB

SHOOT THE GAPS – THE ILB COVERS MIDDLE GAPS
BOTHE OLB'S SUPPORT OFF-TACKLE RUNS AND SWEEPS.

FIG. 5-4A

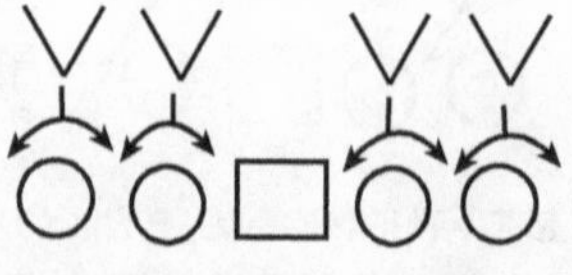

ENGAGE AND READ

FIG. 5-4B

On running plays, outside linebackers must have the speed to stop a sweep and have the quickness to jump inside to stop a running back moving through the line. The most popular play in all levels of football from high school to pee wee is the option play. The option is the first play many offenses learn to run. The option play is really a possibility of four–plays-in-one. With an athletic quarterback, the option is any defensive coordinator's nightmare. The quarterback can either handoff the football, pitch it, run it or even throw it. With your five defenses, I will show you how to best defend the option play. **(See fig. 5-5)**

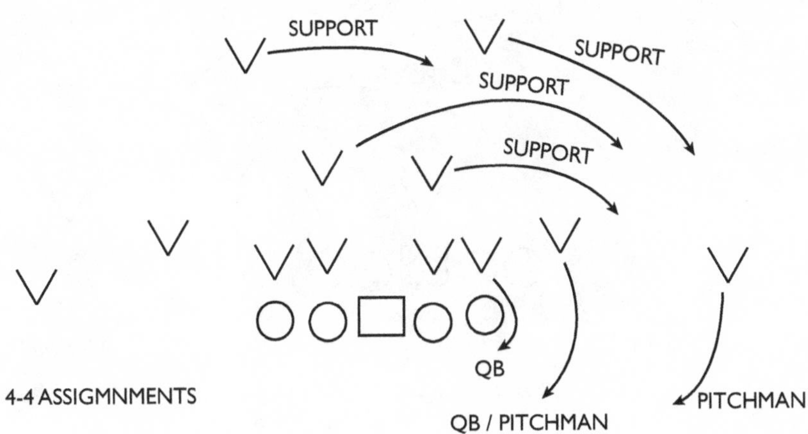

FIG. 5-5

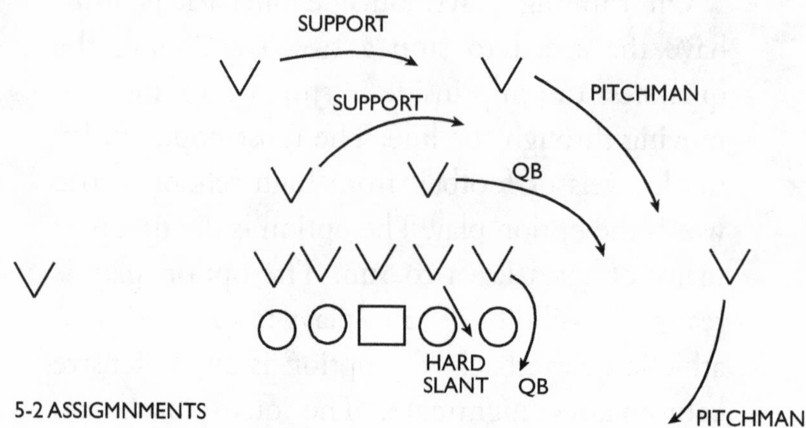

DEFENDING THE OPTION

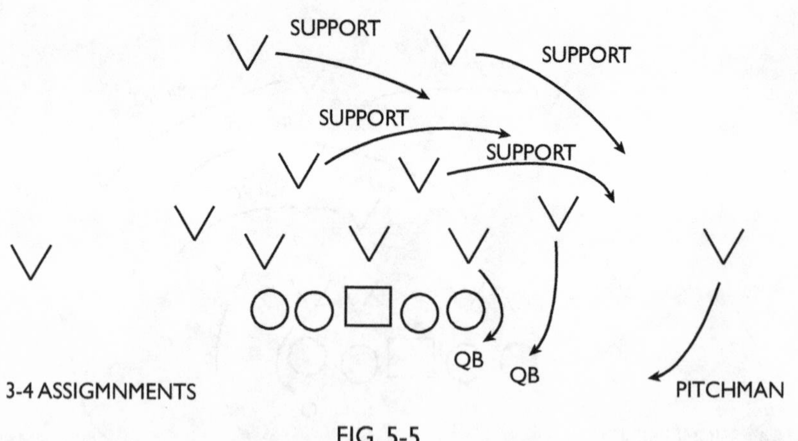

FIG. 5-5

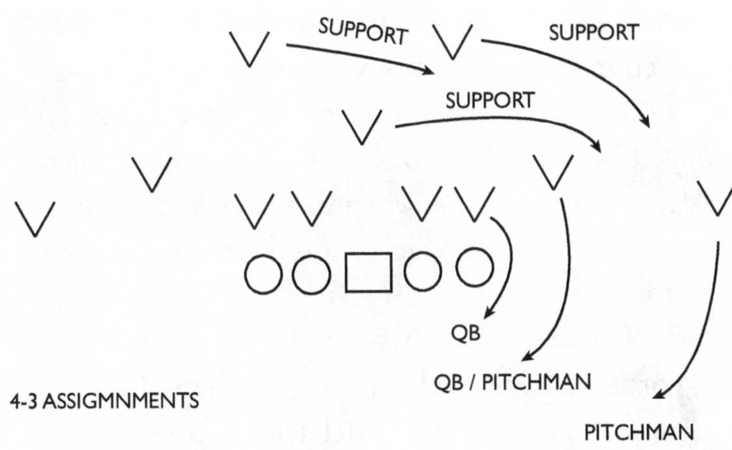

4-3 ASSIGMNMENTS

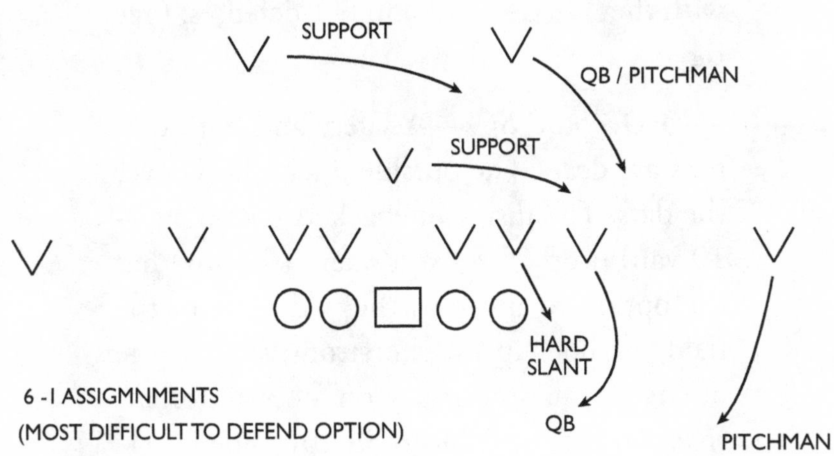

6 -1 ASSIGMNMENTS
(MOST DIFFICULT TO DEFEND OPTION)

As with the simplicity of offensive plays discussed in Chapter 3, keep defensive pass coverage as simple as necessary. *Cover 2*, *3 Deep*, *3 Deep SS Spy*, *Cover 2 Man Under*, *3 Deep Man Under*, *Man to Man* and *Prevent* are the seven basic pass coverage defenses which should suffice for your team:

***Cover 2** – The two safeties are deep. The corners drop back no more than 12-15 yards. The outside linebackers cover the flats. And the inside linebackers drop back 7-10 yards. Cover 2 zone coverage can be used with the 3-4, 4-3, 5-2 and 6-1 defenses. **(See fig. 5-6a)**

***3 Deep SS Spy** – A safety and both corners are deep. The outside linebackers cover the flats. The inside linebackers take their 7-10 yard drop. The extra safety (the spy) has the option to move to the wide side of the field, or line up on the strong side of the offense formation or key on a certain offensive player. The 3 Deep SS Spy zone coverage can be used with the 3-4, 4-3, 5-2 and 6-1 defenses. **(See fig. 5-6b)** A regular **3 Deep** coverage (also with Man Under) can be used with the 4-4.

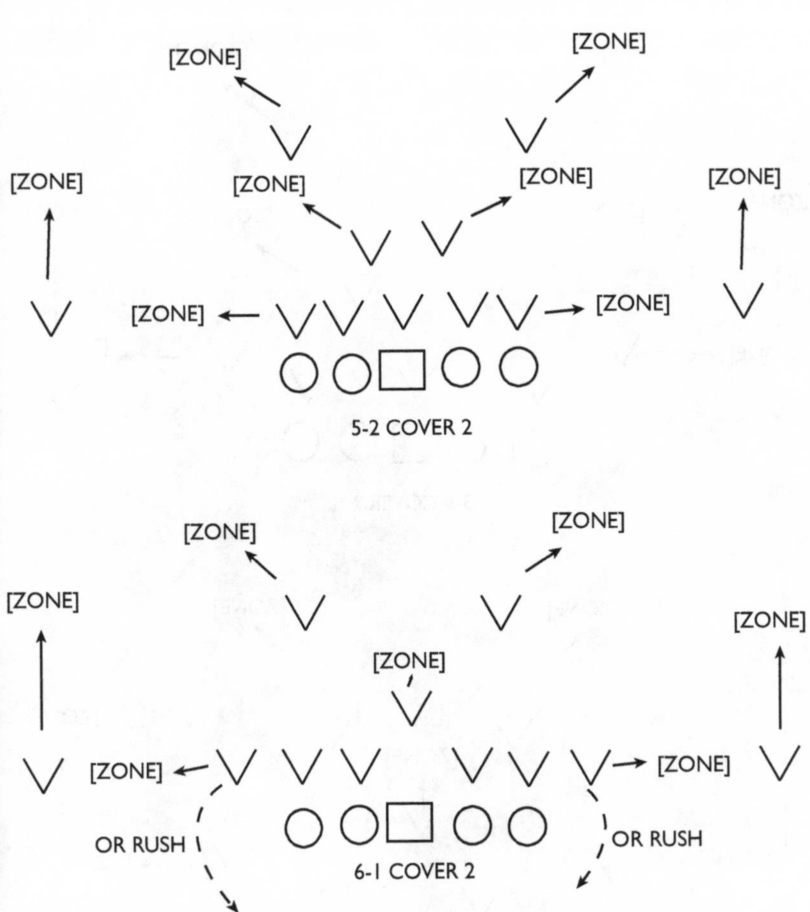
[ZONE]
[ZONE]
[ZONE]
[ZONE]
[ZONE]
[ZONE]
[ZONE]
[ZONE]
5-2 COVER 2
[ZONE]
[ZONE]
[ZONE]
[ZONE]
[ZONE]
[ZONE]
[ZONE]
OR RUSH
OR RUSH
6-1 COVER 2

FIG. 5-6A

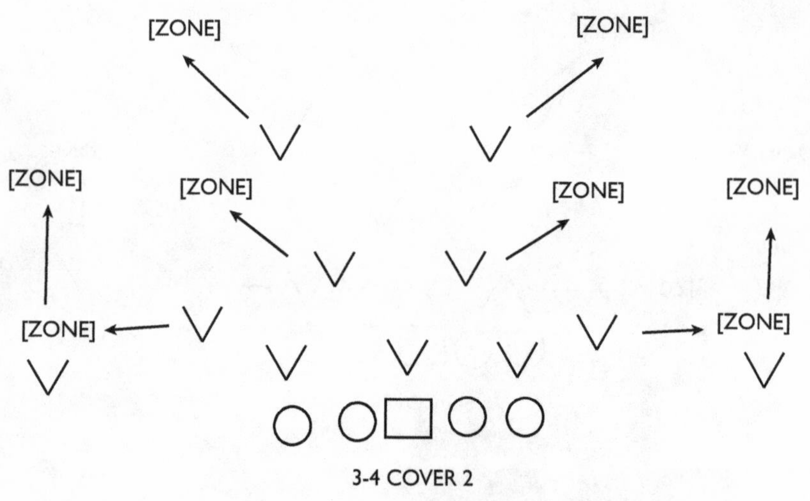

3-4 COVER 2

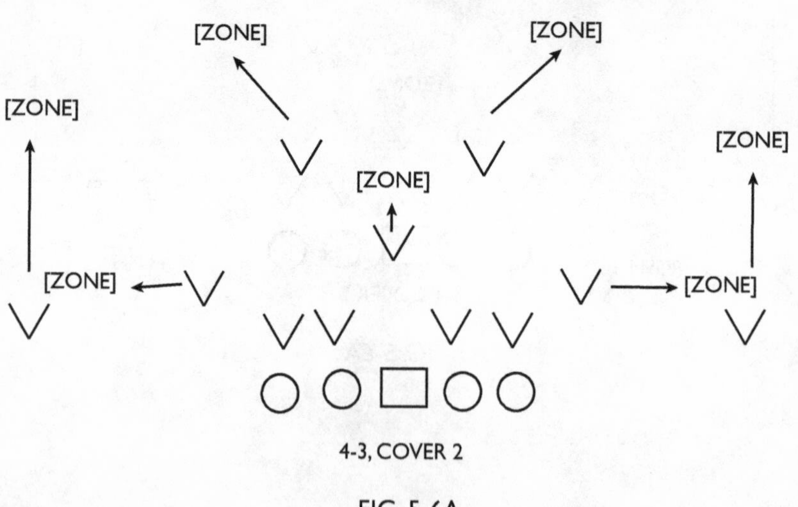

4-3, COVER 2

FIG. 5-6A

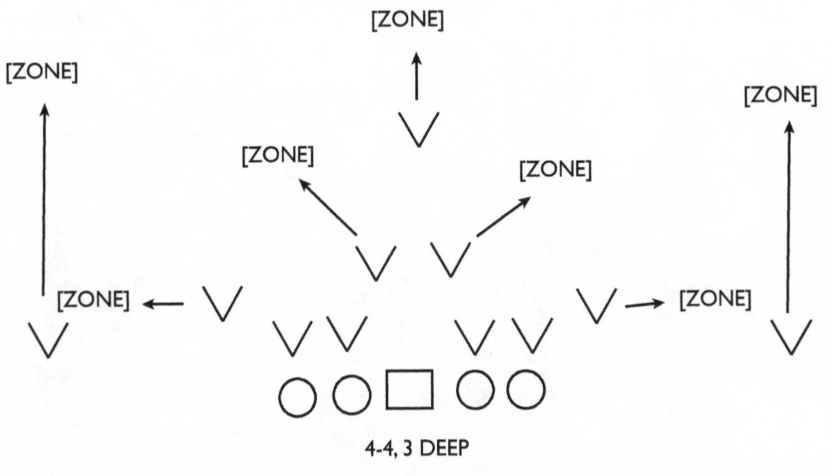

4-4, 3 DEEP

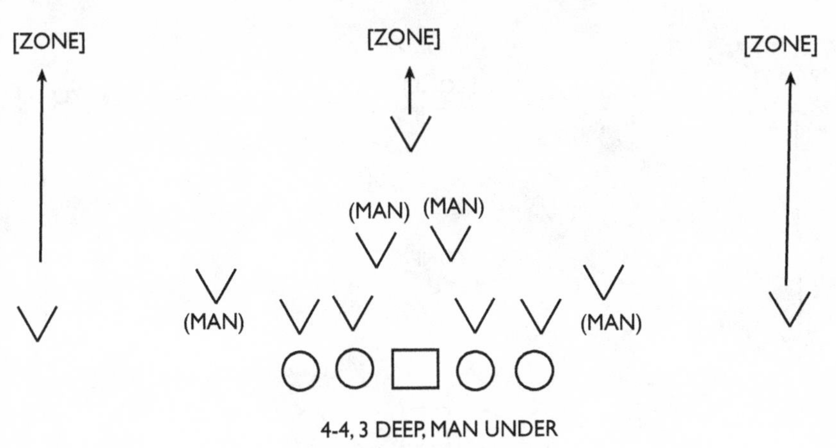

4-4, 3 DEEP, MAN UNDER

FIG. 5-6B

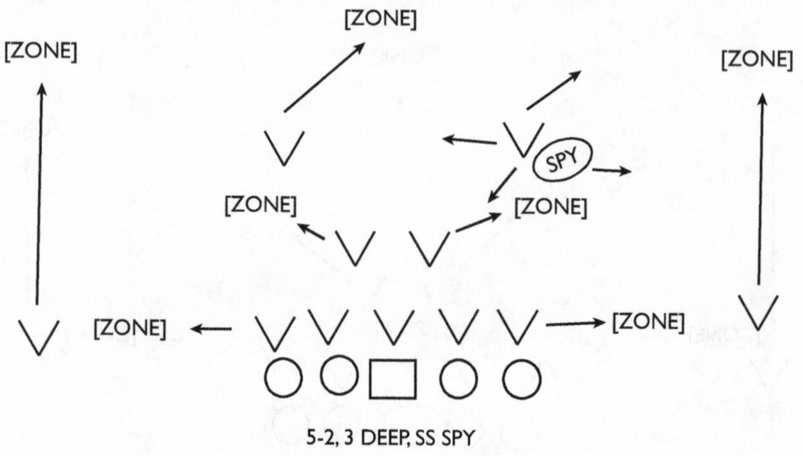

5-2, 3 DEEP, SS SPY

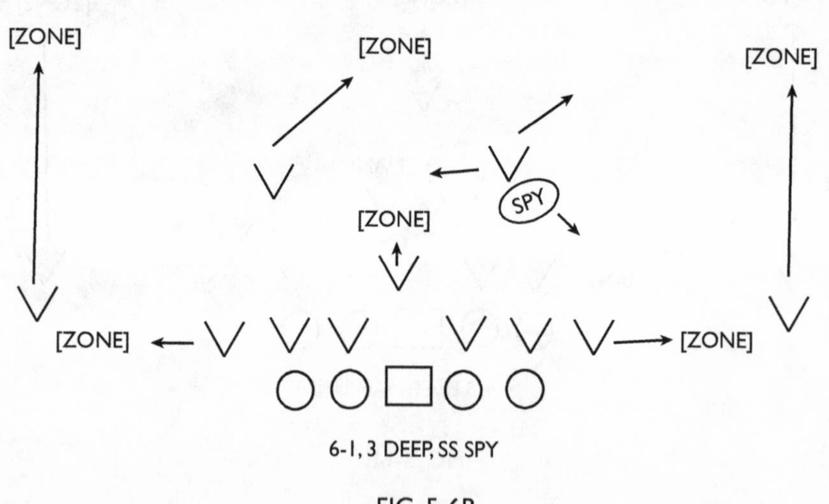

6-1, 3 DEEP, SS SPY

FIG. 5-6B

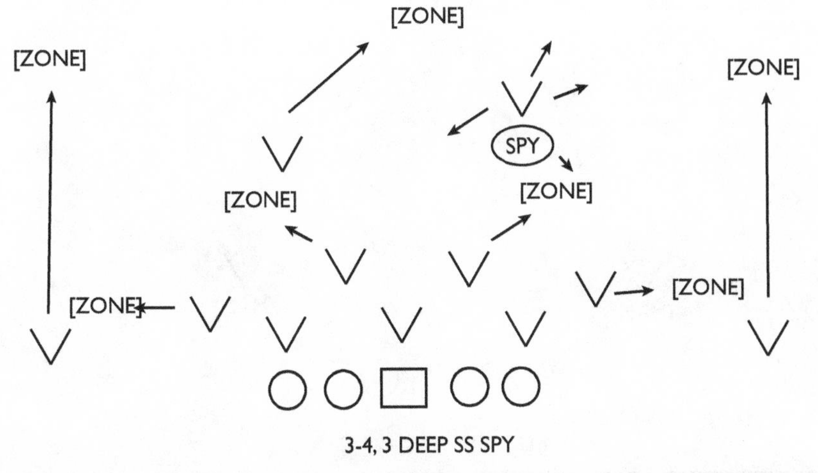

3-4, 3 DEEP SS SPY

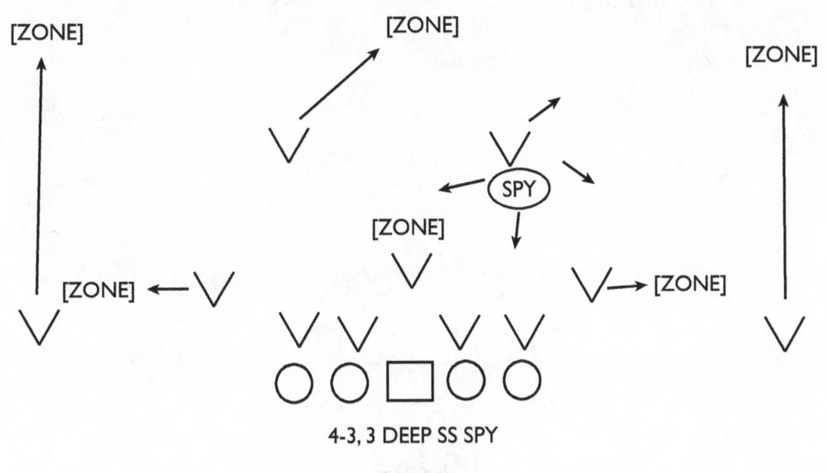

4-3, 3 DEEP SS SPY

FIG. 5-6B

*Cover 2, Man Under – Both safeties are deep with man to man coverage by the corners and linebackers. This coverage works well with 3-4, 4-3, 5-2 and 6-1 defenses. **(See fig. 5-6c)**

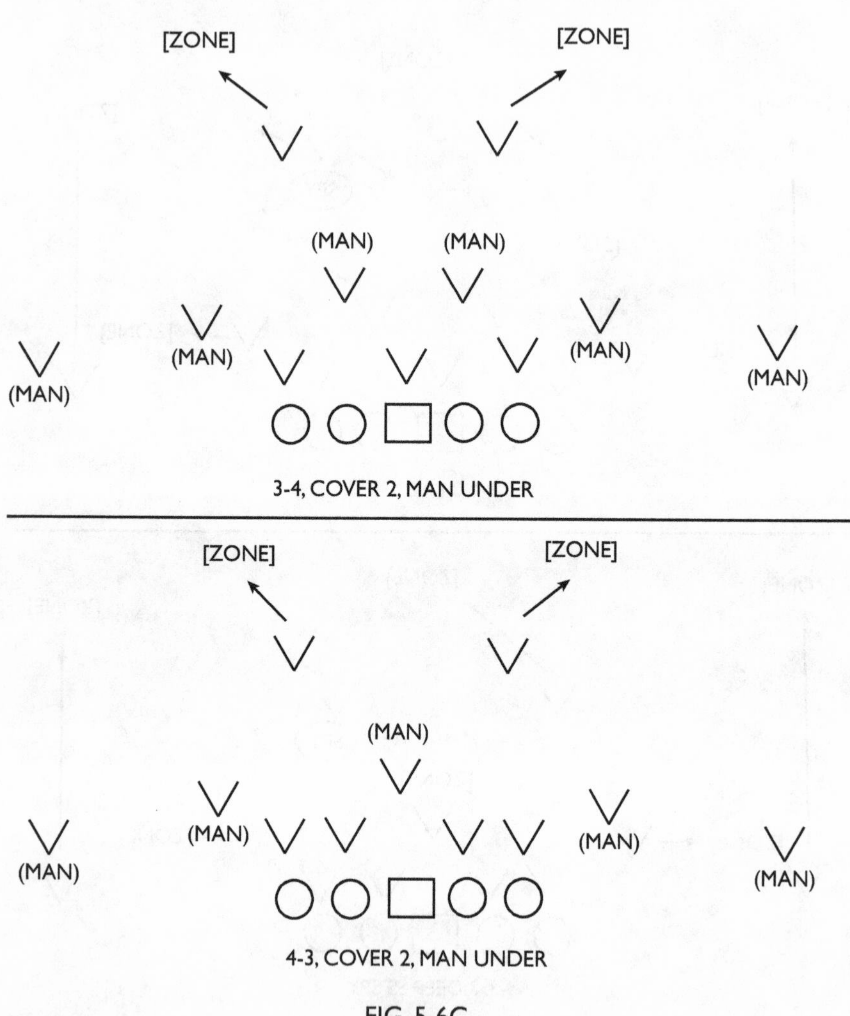
[ZONE]
[ZONE]
(MAN)
(MAN)
(MAN)
(MAN)
(MAN)
(MAN)
3-4, COVER 2, MAN UNDER
[ZONE]
[ZONE]
(MAN)
(MAN)
(MAN)
(MAN)
(MAN)
4-3, COVER 2, MAN UNDER

FIG. 5-6C

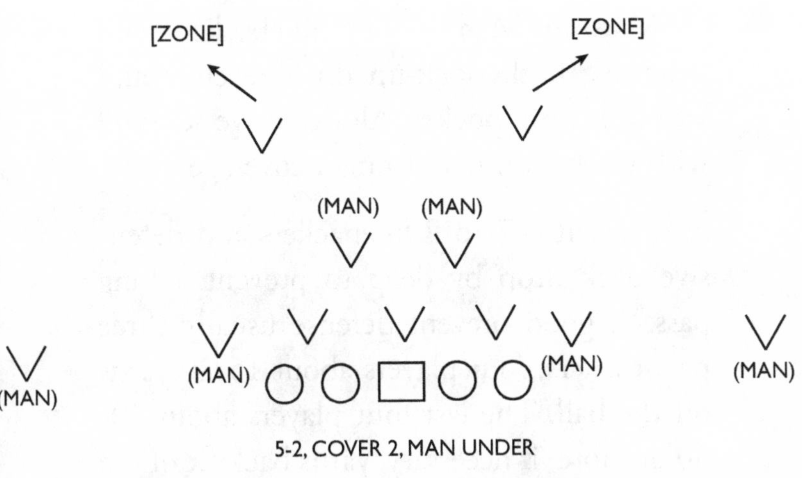

5-2, COVER 2, MAN UNDER

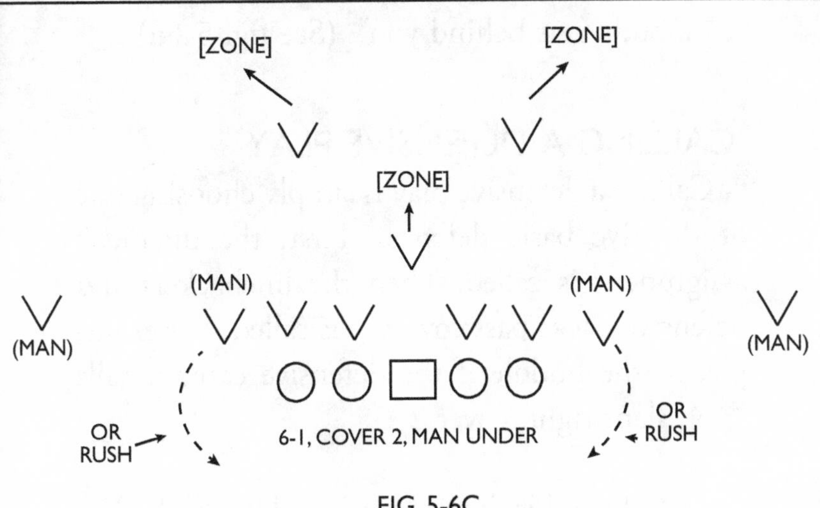

6-1, COVER 2, MAN UNDER

FIG. 5-6C

*__Man to Man__ – The linebackers and defensive backs lock-up on a receiver and stay in his hip pocket. All defensive sets will with work with man to man coverage.

*__Prevent__ – 7 to 8 linebackers and defensive back drop by deep to prevent a long pass. A good prevent defense usually three pass rushers, four players about 15-20 yards off the ball. The last four players about 40-50 or more, if necessary, yards back from the line of scrimmage with the instructions "nobody gets behind you". **(See fig. 5-6d)**

CALLING A DEFENSIVE PLAY

Calling a defensive play is simply choosing one of the five basic defenses. First, the linemen's assignment is called. Then the linebackers and defensive backs pass coverage is called. For example, in the huddle if the defensive captain calls "3-4, slant right, cover 2":

**The 3-4 is the linemen's and linebacker's alignment at the line of scrimmage.

***Slant* tells the linemen and linebackers where they go at the snap of the ball.

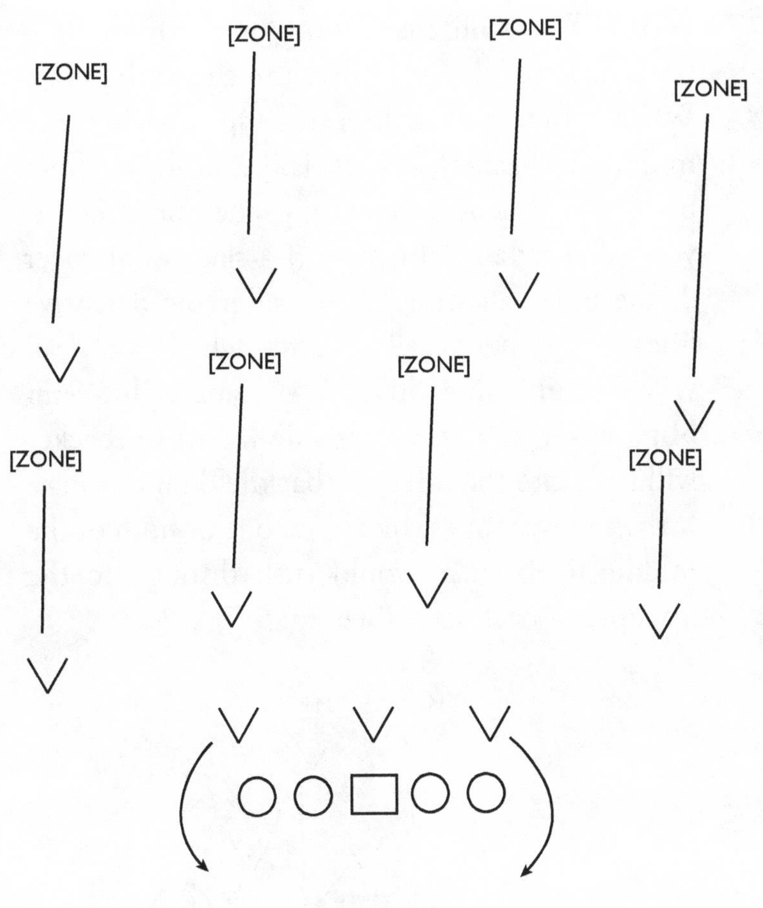

PREVENT DEFENSE

FIG. 5-6D

**And *Cover 2* is the linebackers and defensive backs pass coverage assignments.

BLITZ – A blitz is rushing one or more linebackers across the line of scrimmage at the snap. When calling a blitz, keep it simple. *Mike* is the middle linebacker(s). *Willy* is the weak side linebacker. And *Sam* is the strong side linebacker. If you call a blitz in our play "3-4 slant right cover 2, the blitz call would come after the defensive line's assignment call, "slant right". The call would sound like this: "**3-4, slant right, Sam blitz, cover 2.** The strong side (Sam) linebacker will rush into the offensive backfield on this play. If the call was for a Mike blitz, one or both of the middle linebackers would rush through to the opponent's backfield. **(See fig.** 5-7)

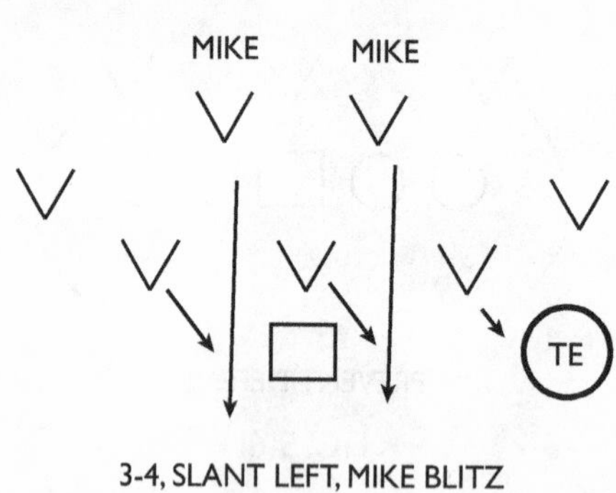

3-4, SLANT LEFT, MIKE BLITZ

FIG. 5-7

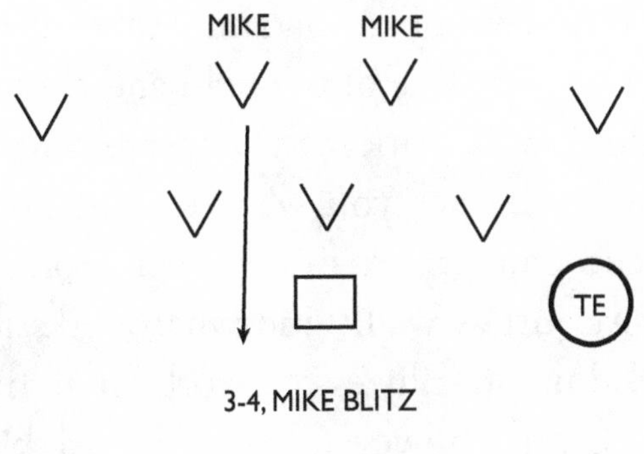

3-4, MIKE BLITZ

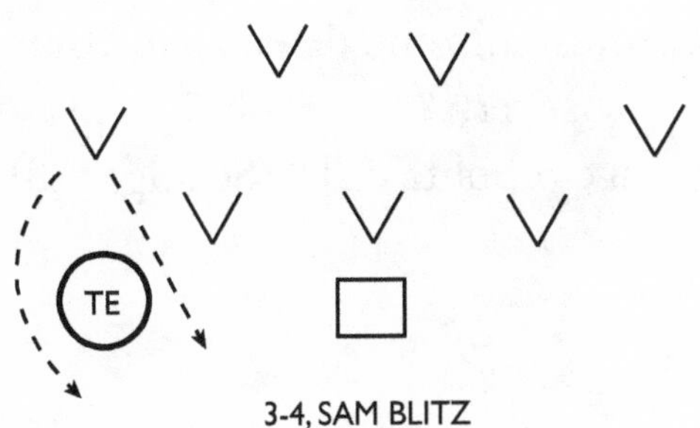

3-4, SAM BLITZ

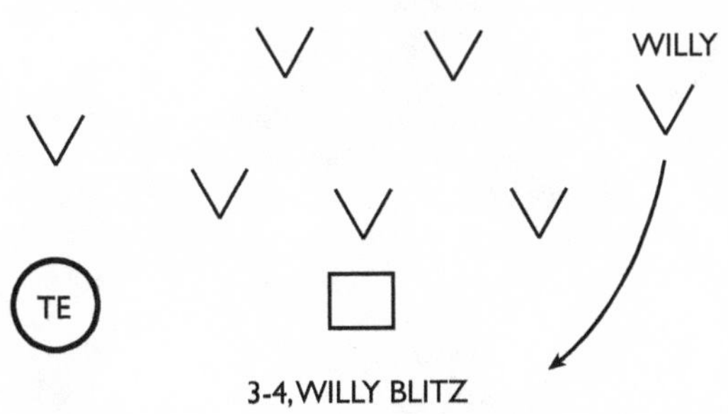

3-4, WILLY BLITZ

FIG. 5-7

If the concept of strong and weak side of a formation or wide side of the field and short side of the field doesn't work for your team, then calling out the linebacker you want to blitz should be sufficient enough. A numeric or alpha system will work just as well. Find what works for your team and use it. Blitzes can work for all five basic defensive sets, however, remember, a blitz is a race to the quarterback before he can release the football. Adjust all zone defenses to cover for the blitzing linebacker(s) or simply just play man to man coverage on blitz calls. **(See fig. 5-8)**

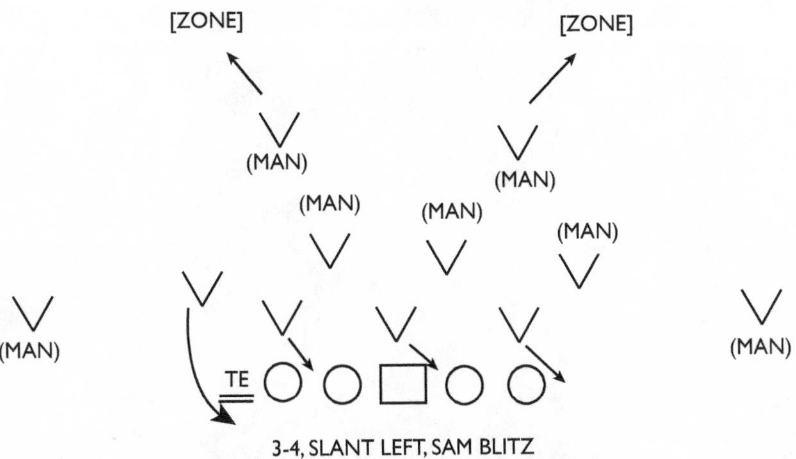

3-4, SLANT LEFT, SAM BLITZ
(MAN TO MAN OR COVER 2 MAN UNDER)

[ZONE] [ZONE]

[ZONE] [ZONE]

[ZONE] [ZONE]

[ZONE] [ZONE]

TE

3-4, SLANT LEFT, SAM BLITZ, COVER 2

NOTE: THE RIGHT ILB COVER THE AREA USUALLY COVERED BY THE BLITZING SAM LINEBACKER.

FIG. 5-8

SIX
AUDIBLES

If you have a quarterback who is comfortable with your offensive plays and is proficient enough to run it, you might want to allow him to use audibles. An audible is changing the play at the line of scrimmage than what was called in the huddle. Even at the elementary level, changing a play at the line of scrimmage is sometimes necessary.

To assist your quarterback, make your audible system as simple as possible. If a 26 Veer is called in the huddle and your QB sees the defense stacked to the side of the play, there's a good chance that the 26 Veer will gain little yards, if any at all. In this situation, maybe a 37 Toss Sweep would work better. The quarterback shouts out "**check-zero**" twice to both sides. This alerts his team that a change in the play is coming. On a running play, the audible call is the play number in reverse. The 37 Toss Sweep would be 7, **3, Tommy Sally** (the "T" in Tommy represents "Toss", the "S" in Sally represents "Sweep", of course you can use any name or signals or just use 7, 3 or 7-Tommy or 3-Sally. For further simplicity, do not change the receiver or backfield alignments unless it's necessary for the new play to run effectively. The whole idea of an audible is to gain an advantage, either a man advantage or a wide side of the field advantage. So just call the audible and run the play. Later on, you might want to get creative and change alignments when using audibles. As long as your players can understand and execute audibles and formations then have at it.

If the same 26 Veer is called in the huddle, then at the line of scrimmage your quarterback sees that the defense is over loaded to his right side, your QB can just run the same play to the opposite side, making it a 25 Veer. The quarterback would "check-zero" twice then yell "pop" twice. "Pop" means to run the same play on the opposite side (or call 5, 2, Viceroy – V for Veer). If your running backs are pro formation and the QB wants them in the I formation, he should just turn to them and tell him where he wants them. Do the same with the tight end. Go tap him on the butt if necessary to get his attention. For the wide outs, yelling to where he wants them positioned and/or hand gestures should do.

Basic audibles on pass plays should suffice as well. Pass play audibles are called straight up. The quarterback will say "check-zero" twice to both sides and then bark out the pass routes twice in x, y, and z order. If the QB calls 9, 4, 8, then of course, the SE runs a Fly pattern. The TE runs a Drag route, and the FL runs a Post. The backfield would shift to the Pro formation to help out with pass protection. Also a designated back or the back to the wide side of the field could float to the flats as a safety valve receiver for your quarterback to throw to if none of his three primary receivers are open. **(See fig. 6-1)**

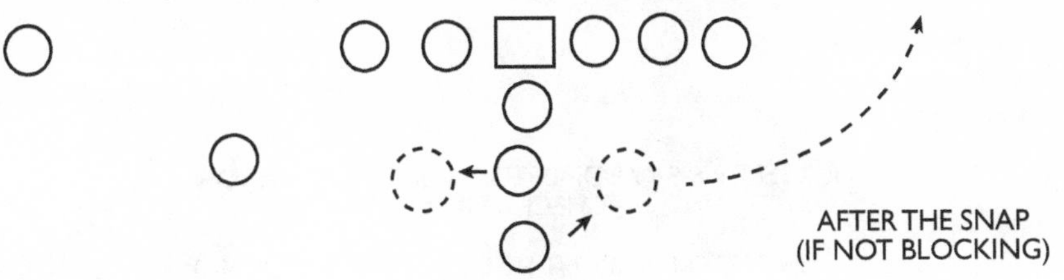

34 BLAST - AUDIBLE TO: 8-7-4
(CHECK-ZERO)

(ON AN AUDIBLE FROM RUNNING PLAY TO PASS PLAY HAVE YOUR BACKS SHIFT TO THE PRO FORMATION TO HELP OUT WITH PASS PROTECTION.)

FIG. 6-1

If audibilizing from a pass play to a running play use the opposite numbers for your running play. If your quarterback wants to change the called pass play 8, 6, 9 to the running play 34

Isolation he would "check-zero" then call 4, 3 Ike (I – for Isolation) or just simply 4, 3. And since the 34 Isolation is usually run from the "I" formation, your running backs would shift to it on the call. And if the tight end is on the left side, he would simply shift over to the right side of the formation. **(See fig. 6-2)**

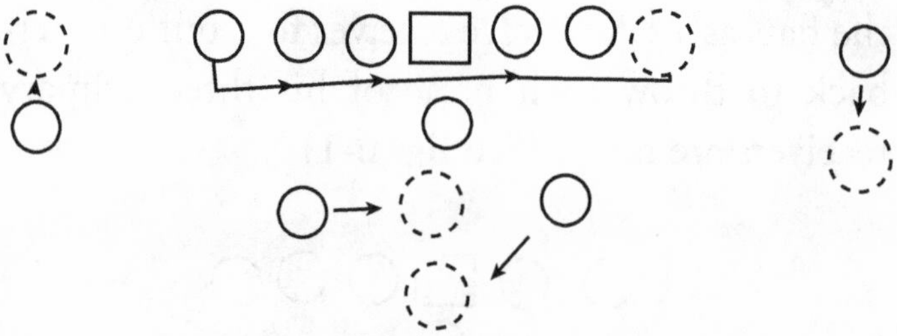

PRO, LEFT, 8-6-9 – AUDIBLE TO: 4, 3, IKE (34 ISOLATION) (CHECK-ZERO)

(TE SHIFTS TO THE RIGHT SIDE TO AID IN BLOCKING)

FIG. 6-2

SEVEN
SPECIAL TEAMS

It is never too early to work on special teams. Summer is the time to do just that. Find out who's a special teams type of player along with the kicker, punter and long snapper you found earlier during the summer pre-pads drills. Keep in mind that kicking, punting and place kicking are three different skills. One person cannot always both kick and punt. Take the time to find the right fit. If necessary, grab a player from the soccer team and have him kick for you. Long snapping is a special skill, as well, which requires a lot of practice. Chances are good that there is a long-snapper on your squad. Flush him out!

PLACE KICKING

On field goals and the point after touchdown (PAT), your kicker is going to have to be able to lift the ball quickly over outstretched hands of defenders from just about seven yards from the line of scrimmage. One exercise is to place 4 or 5 dummies about

6 yards in front of your kicker and have him kick over them, practicing his lift and getting use to kicking with obstructions in the way. Another drill is to have players with smaller pads rush the kicker from each corner and pull back at the last second. This exercise with help him concentrate on kicking the ball while filtering out distractions. Concentration and confidence are your kicker's best weapons to kick effectively.

Your kicker should constantly work on his mechanics which are spotting the ball, keeping his head down, his approach, jamming his plant foot firmly on the ground and follow-through with his kicking leg. Once your kicker has a consistent grasp on his mechanics, then start practicing kicking for accuracy and distance.

Find a holder for your place kicks. He needs to able to kneel comfortably, have good, soft hands to catch the football from the long snapper, set it on the tee and spin the laces away from the kicker. And do all of this in less than two seconds. Note: avoid using your starting quarterback or any other key players. Holders are in a vulnerable position and could easily get hurt if someone runs into him. There is an excellent holder on your squad sitting on the bench. Find him!

BLOCKING PROTECTION FOR KICKS

Practice field goal and PAT protection every chance you get. It is not as easy as it may appear on televised college or pro games. On all plays from scrimmage, offensive linemen either attack on running plays or retreat in pass protection. The blocking scheme for place kicks is somewhere in the middle.

On field goal and PAT protection, the front seven must stand their ground and not allow any defensive penetration. An interlocking stance is very important for this protection. From the center the guards place a foot inside the center's foot from behind. The tackles place a foot inside the each guard's foot also from behind. And the tight ends place a foot inside each tackles' foot from behind. Both wingmen set on each end of the formation places a foot next to each tight end and stand at a 45 degree angle in a ready or breakdown position. This blocking technique will be difficult for most players. It requires solid upper body and leg strength. Find those players who can block using this technique well. Look down your depth chart. You will find players able and more than willing to play this important role for your team. **(See fig. 7-1)**

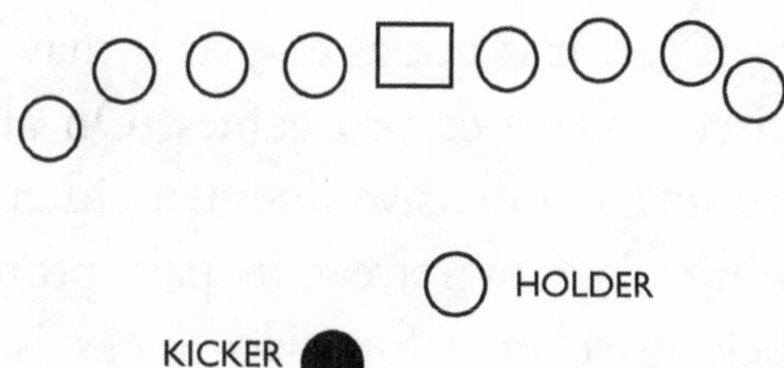

FIG. 7-1

PUNT

The action of punting a football consist of taking a step forward with the non-kicking foot, dropping the ball horizontally and striking of top of the kicking foot.

Finding a punter may be more difficult to find. Not every kicker can punt a football. Punting may be the most challenging to teach a player. Punting a football correctly requires a lot of punting. Ball placement, foot positioning and leg extension are essential for consistent punts. Again, during the summer have your punter just punt the ball. Have him get use to get use to the feel of the ball, the placement of the football and leg follow through extension.

Once you are satisfied with the height and distance of your punters punts, place two large dummy bags three yards in front of your punter and three yards apart. He should step towards the dummies has he steps into his kick. Between every other kick, move the dummies closer together and closer to the punter until he is punting the ball between an 18-inch to two-foot space with consistency. Then have players with hand-held dummy pads run toward the punter at an angle. Have them pass the kicker just as he punts the ball. These and similar drills will help your kickers get comfortable, gain confidence and be more efficient to execute solid kicks under pressure.

Punt team protection calls for players agile enough to hold blocks effectively, then release, sprinting downfield to cover the punt and make tackles. These players will be easier to find. Usually, punt teams consist of linebackers, defensive backs, wide receivers and running backs. The success of your punt team revolves around having a rhythm. There is the snap; the step with the plant foot; and the punt. One way to achieve rhythm is to have your players hold their blocks 3 to 4 second counts then release downfield. Or have them release downfield when they hear the sound of the punt. Find the rhythm best suited for your punt unit, and then sharpen it. Remember, repetition is the key. **(See fig.** 7-2)

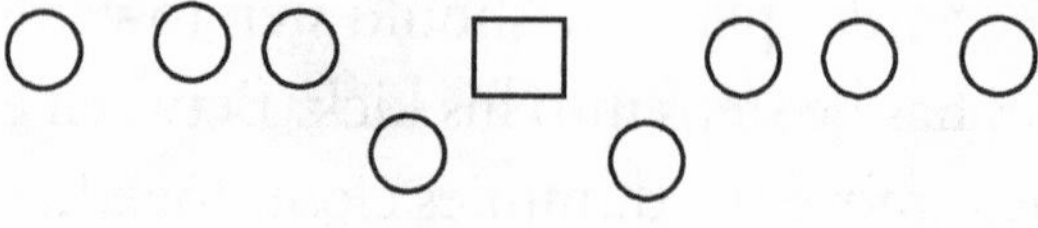

REGULAR PUNT FORMATION

FIG. 7-2

PUNT RETURN

Your punt return team will definitely require guys who are quick, agile, versatile and most importantly, disciplined. It's just the opposite of the punt squad. For this group you need guys who can hold up the offense at the line of scrimmage; rush the punter when necessary; then guys who can quickly drop back to set up a blocking line for the return man.

Discipline is needed to not block the opposing team in the back or clip during this transition of ball possession. This is no easy task. A play from scrimmage in all levels of football is fast-paced for the given level. Split-second decisions are made on every play. The decision to block or not requires focus as well as discipline. *An easy rule of thumb is if you cannot see an opposing player's front number, don't block him.*

PUNT PRACTICE

Also practice blocking punts during your special teams sessions. Teach a few of your kamikaze guys on the punt return team the proper angles to take to block punt without missing the football or roughing the kicker. Find a stand-in for your regular punter, usually a non-starting player. After the snap, have him punt a count or two slower than normal. Allow your kamikazes to block punts using proper punt block techniques which include extended arms, open hands and face down to avoid having the ball hit them in the throat. When you're satisfied with your punt blockers' progress, have the stand-in punter speed up his rhythm one-half count. And repeat. (See fig. 7-3)

Find a good punt return player. Don't fool around with this position. Use your better players for this position. Fumbling the football on a punt return usually determines the outcomes of games. It's the one turnover your team may not recover from. The three "goods" are essential qualities for a punt return player. *Good hands* for catching the football. *Good vision* for seeing the

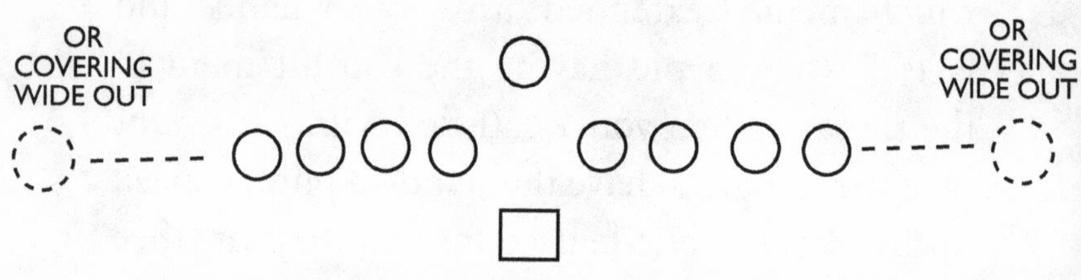

REGULAR PUNT RETURN FORMATION

FIG. 7-3

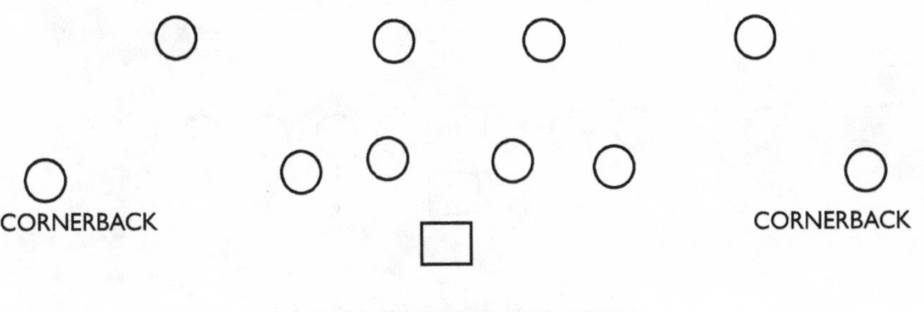

SAFE PUNT RETURN FORMATION

FIG. 7-3

RETURN MAN

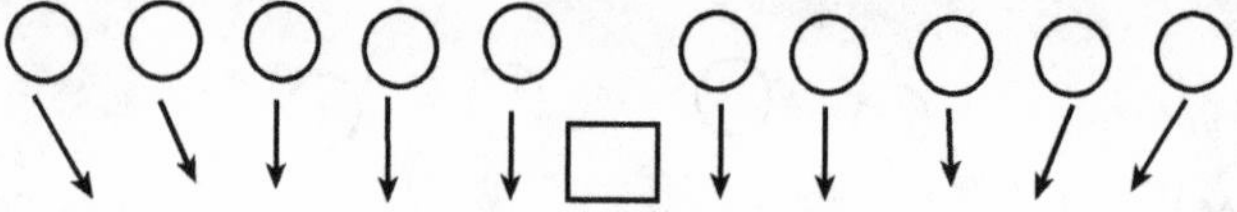

PUNT BLOCK FORMATION

FIG. 7-3

whole field. And *good judgment* for making sound decisions like when to catch the ball and run, or call a fair catch or when to back away and let the football hit the ground.

KICK OFF

Running towards the football and kicking it from a tee is not an easy thing to do. The approach, keeping eyes on the football, kicking the ball square and the follow-through are most important. At the beginning of summer drills just let your kicker just kick the football. Let him get use to approaching the ball and kicking emphasizing his plant foot and follow-through. For kickoffs, distance and placement are important factors. Once you are satisfied with your kicker's kickoff distance, then you can practice angling kicks to different areas downfield.

KICK OFF COVERAGE

To me, kickoff coverage is the most important phase of special teams. If your team is not efficient and cannot execute in this area of the game, you're going to be in for a long and bitter season. Good kickoff coverage play will not only give your team field position but can give you a psychological edge as well. A dominant kickoff coverage team tells your opponents not only did you just score, and now you're going to give them the ball, pinning them down deep in their territory. It is crucial to practice kickoff coverage until you are satisfied that your team is executing it properly. Then practice it some more. If your kickoff team is not intense in practice, they won't be excited come game time.

There are various ways to cover kickoffs. There's the traditional "stay-in-you-lane" approach with a designated safety trail man. The "braided", "weave" or "zigzag" attack is when players run criss-cross down the field with the player next to them. And the "staggered start" is when every other player lines up 5 yards ahead or behind the next player. (**See fig.** 7-4) All of these approaches are designed, of course, to confuse and disrupt the blocking of the other team.

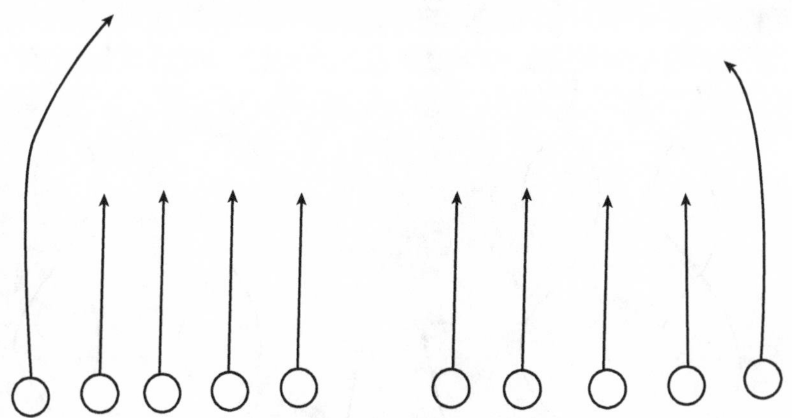

REGULAR KICKOFF COVERAGE

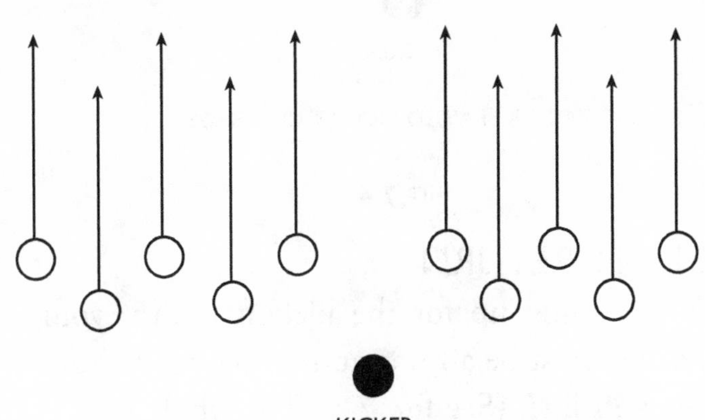

STAGGERED KICKOFF COVERAGE

FIG. 7-4

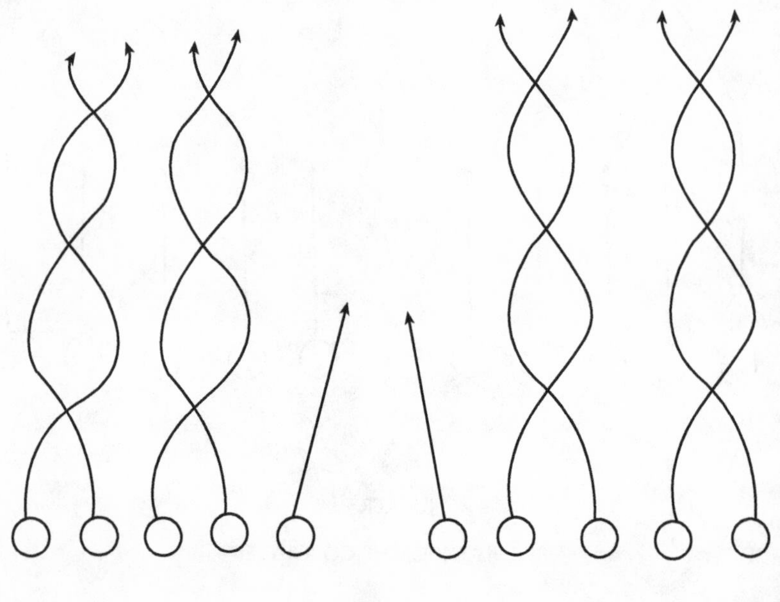

ZIG-ZAG OR BRAIDED KICKOFF COVERAGE

FIG. 7-4

KICKOFF RETURN

When lining up for the kickoff return, your front line must be a minimum of ten yards from the kickoff line. (**See fig.** 7-5) The whole field is at your disposal during the kickoff return. Return left, return right, or return up the middle. You can run reverses, double reverses, laterals or even throw-back across the field laterals.

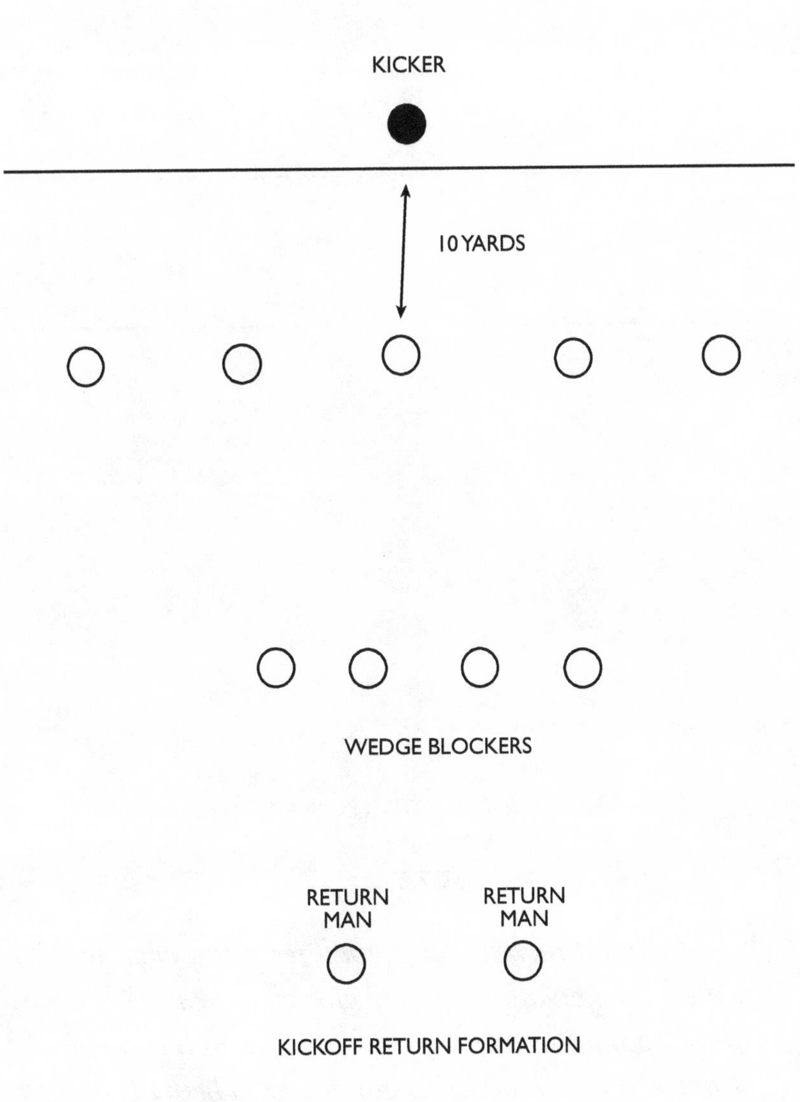

KICKOFF RETURN FORMATION

FIG. 7-5

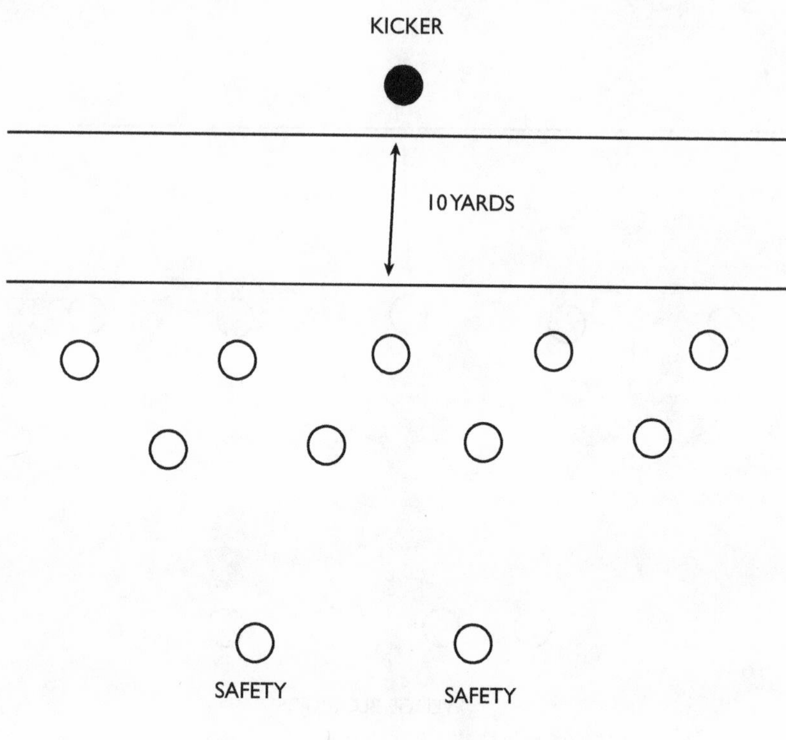

ONSIDE KICKOFF RETURN FORMATIONS

FIG. 7-5

My junior high school football team ran what we called the "huddle play" on kickoff returns. When the deep man received the football, the entire return team ran and huddled around him. The ball was handed to several players during the huddle or the first man just kept the football. Just before the kick-off team would get to our huddle, the huddle dispersed and we ran in 11 different directions with all of us pretending to have the football. You are receiving the football. Be creative. The kickoff return gives your team a chance to dictate your field position to start your next drive. Take advantage of it.

ONSIDE KICKOFF

The onside kickoff is a desperation attempt to get the ball from the kickoff, usually late in the game. Practice it. Practice it. If your kicker is solely a kicker and plays no other position, all throughout every practice session he should be mastering the art of directional kickoffs and onside kickoffs.

There is nothing more heartbreaking than to watch a team who is trailing late in a game and needs to recover an onside kick, but doesn't have a clue of how to execute it. Always give your team a chance to win. Practice. Practice all facets of the game. Practice the onside kick. **(See fig.** 7-6)

There is no exact way to kick for the onside kick. Many teams use the high bounce approach, the end over end kick, squib kick (rumble ball) or the ricochet (kicking the ball hard at the nearest opponent and hoping the ball hits one of them and comes back towards the kicking team) approach to recover the onside kick. Be creative

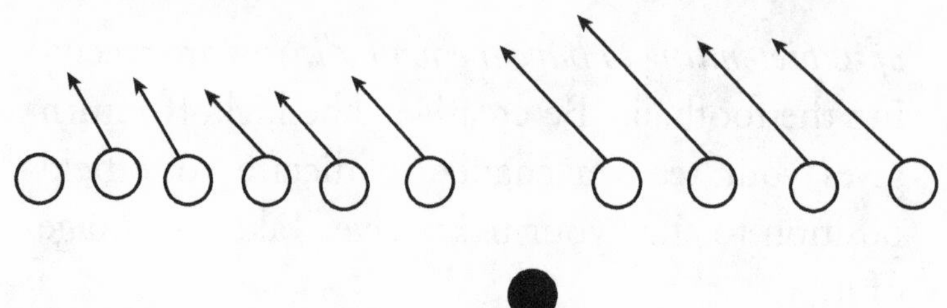

ONSIDE KICKOFF FORMATIONS

FIG. 7-6

and come up with other ways to recover the onside kick. It's up to you. Remember: the football has to travel 10 yards or is touch by the opposing team before your team can recover it.

EIGHT
PRACTICE

An old maxim says "practice makes perfect". I would amend that to "practice creates excellence". There is no such thing as perfection, however, excellence allows players to operate at a high efficiency level while allowing for human error and miscues. In your practices, you should strive for excellence during every session.

TEACHING THE GAME

For Pee Wee, junior high and recreational football leagues, it's a good idea to start practices as early as you can before the beginning of your first game. Kids in these leagues are usually new to the game. A lot of instruction will most likely be necessary. Some will know the game of football. Some will have a working knowledge of the sport. And some will know very little about the game. As head coach, you are going to have to teach the game of football to your players. You will not only teach the fundamentals, but you will have to teach every aspect of the game, from basic player positions to the concept of offense, defense and the kicking game to the rules of the game to fair conduct on the field. Take as much time as it is necessary to teach the game of football to your young players. Chances are they watch football on Saturdays and Sundays. Most players will catch on quickly.

For high school, you should implore your returning players to find time during the off-season to lift weights and conduct conditioning workouts on their own. Not only does this show initiative on the part of your players, but it will save valuable time when the official summer drills begin. It's a good idea to schedule weightlifting during summer drills as well.

FIRST PRACTICES

Good structure of practice sessions is essential for starting off the season on and positive and productive note. *At my high school in Michigan, back in the 1970s, we started summer practices a week after the 4th of July holiday. They weren't really "practices", more like workouts three days a week. No equipment, of course, just shorts and cleats. It was conditioning. There was lot of running, exercising and stretching with not a football in sight for six weeks.* Each league and school district has specific rules on when you can run practices with body equipment. Know the rules!

Two weeks before the issuance of full equipment, my coach gave out helmets. You should too, if possible. Let them get used to wearing it. Try to make sure that the helmets fit each player correctly. For many players in pee wee, recreational and junior high leagues, it may be the first time they put a real football helmet on their heads. This can be a chore for rocket league and pee wee league players. Players need to get use to wearing their helmets. *My high school coaches used the emersion method when it came to wearing our helmets. They would not let anyone take their helmets off for any reason throughout any practice session. He made it a challenge to us. Looking back, that approach was quite beneficial.* A seemingly small thing like keeping on a helmet fostered a tradition of discipline that translated to our play on the field. (You should, however, allow younger players in pee wee, rocket and junior high to remove their helmets from time to time during practices.)

At this time you may want to introduce the football to your practices. Break into two units, backs and linemen. With just helmets and shoes, this is the time to mainly work on appropriate arm and footwork techniques and all the while still focusing on exercise, stretching and running (sprints and distances). The linemen can work on body positioning along with pass protection and defensive swerve techniques. Agility drills for both offensive and defensive backs. Many running backs need to be taught to properly receive a handoff and carry a football. Tip drills for defensive backs and linebackers will keep them alert and have a nose for the football.

It's always a good idea to start working on your kicking game right away. Find out who can place kick, kick off, punt, long-snap and hold for field goals and for the point after touchdown. During these practices, just long-snap, punt, place kick and kickoff... a lot.

During these two weeks of technique and conditioning, feel free to implement a few basic plays towards the end of practice. Just walk through some plays, using positioning with linemen. New and first-time players will greatly benefit from seeing plays in a walk-through mode before putting on pads.

PRACTICING WITH PADS

The first day of full pads can be very exciting. Most players are itching to hit somebody after weeks of conditioning and drills. Sometimes coaches can get more excited than the players and are quite anxious to start hitting, that they'll start scrimmages directly after warm ups. Resist that urge. Instead, spend the entire practice, if necessary, teaching proper and safe blocking and tackling. Then ease into full scrimmages.

Remember to keep stressing technique. Technique will now be more difficult with full pads on your players. Watch for equipment problems, and get them corrected immediately. All equipment should fit as best as possible. Wear all equipment properly with all pads intact. Monitor your players. Nowadays, the trend is for players to wear thinner than required hip, thigh and knee pads, no mouth piece or even no pads on certain areas of their body. Don't play that game. If a player does not wear all required equipment, it's your responsibility to not let him practice. With that being said, most, if not all, school districts and state laws require all high school and recreation players to wear full equipment and proper pads for the body.

With full pads, you can now break off into the individual units; offensive and defensives linemen, running backs, receivers, linebackers and defensive backs. The first week or two, unit work should be 60-75% of your practice. Scrimmages should make up about 25% of practice. During scrimmages is the time to focus on your playbook. Run your basic core offense and defense plays, over and over and over again.

Again, monitor your players. Is your quarterback's mechanics sound? Does he take the snap from center correctly and with confidence? Does he pivot appropriately for the called play? Does he hand off properly and carry out his fakes? How is he on the option and tosses? Check your quarterback's passing and how he sets up. Is he throwing over hand or side arm?

Are your running backs receiving handoffs securely and hitting the holes crisply? How are their fakes? Do they block well? Can they competently receive passes out of the backfield?

How about your receivers? Can they catch the football consistently with their hands and not with their bodies? Do they run sharp, crisp routes? Can they block effectively downfield without holding the defender or pushing in the back? Do they hustle back to the huddle after a long incomplete pass?

Monitor your offensive linemen. Does your O-Line break the huddle with authority and jog to the line of scrimmage every time? (*My high school offensive line coach insisted on always jogging to the line. "Mentally, especially in the 4th quarter", he said, "It tells the defensive line we're still coming at you".)* Test your offensive linemen. Do they run block well? Do they fire off the line on each running play? Are they driving their legs when engaging the defender? Can your guards pull and block on sweeps and reverses? How's their pass protection? Is their stance wide enough for proper pass protection? Check their footwork. Do they keep a wide, balanced base? Do they sustain their blocks?

Check your entire defensive unit. Are they using proper technique at each position? Are they tackling with the proper form technique? Do they tackle well with face up and using arms to wrap up? Do they react well to the flow of the play? Do they rally to the football? (*The hallmark of Bo Schembechler's defenses, in his 20 years as head football coach at the University of Michigan, was that at the end of every play there were no less than seven defensive players near the football).* That's rallying to the ball!

Are your defensive linemen staying true to their technique? Can they defeat the double team block effectively? Do they use their shoulders properly to gain a leverage advantage? Can each member of your D-line occupy two offensive linemen to free up your linebackers to make tackles?

Are your linebackers filling the holes quickly on running plays? Do they hustle laterally parallel to the line of scrimmage on sweeps and options? Do they drop back into pass coverage with the correct depth? Can they cover a running back in man to man situations?

Are your cornerbacks and safeties supporting against running plays? How is their man to man coverage? Do they have enough speed and quickness for those positions? Do they react well to the ball in zone coverage?

Take full advantage of your scrimmage sessions by purposely calling plays that force both offensive and defensive players to use the techniques taught in your unit drills. Run double team blocks, gaps and straight on blocking. Evaluate both offensive and defensive linemen. Unit drills and live scrimmages are different. See if your players can make that transition effectively.

Test your linebackers. Run sweeps and options to see how they flow and react laterally across the line of scrimmage and support against the run. Run halfback isolations between the tackles to see how your backers fill a whole and analyze how they step into a block. Are your linebackers attacking the blocker, or are they waiting to get blocked?

Test your defensive backs. In pass coverage, use man to man, zone, man under and press coverage. Run sweeps, options and running plays between the tackles to see how they stop the run.

An excellent way to gauge how well your defense reacts to the football is to run draws, screens, reverses, counters and deep passes. If your defense consistently reacts well to these plays, they will rarely give up the big play.

Test your offensive linemen. Do they run block well? Are they driving their legs when engaging the defender? Can your guards pull and block on sweeps and reverses? How's their pass protection? Check their footwork. Do they keep a wide, balanced base?

OFFENSIVE DRILLS AND TECHNIQUES

Quarterbacks - Teach your QB how to throw the football. The best way and the easiest way to do this is to watch how he throws, then work on his mechanics without totally changing his throwing motion. First, have him grip the football correctly with the laces between his fingers. Next position the football in a comfortable position just before he rears back to throw. He can hold it near his ear, near his upper chest or near his back shoulder as he drops back the pass. Now watch his release. Is he throwing over hand or side-arm? Is he following through or is his arm stopping too soon after the release? Watch is foot work. Is he pushing off properly on his plant (back) foot? Continue watching your quarterback and adjust things as necessary until you are satisfied with how your QB sets up, steadies his feet, releases and follows through.

After your quarterback(s) has mastered how to properly throw the football, teach him to throw certain types of passes. Out patterns, screen passes and crossing (in) patterns are the hardest passes your quarterback will have the throw. Quickness and accuracy is crucial for completion of these passes. Any mistakes on these throws usually results in an interception for the other team. Out patterns take a strong arm to throw it efficiently and effectively. Screen passes takes a lot of touch on the throw…and sometimes, depending on the rush of the defensive line, the pass must be lofted over the defensive linemen's outstretch arms. Crossing or in patterns are difficult because it's trying to hit a lateral moving target. Your QB must be able to lead the football to his moving receiver. Your quarterbacks must have keen concentration and be able to spot their receiver through the maze of bodies and hands swiping at the ball.

Handing off the football is not as easy as it might appear in college and pro football games. Teach your quarterback an efficient way to hand the ball off. There is a rhythm and a method. The number one rule is that the QB does not release the ball until it is firmly in the stomach of his back. Repetition. Repetition.

Receiving the snap from center takes a lot of practice. Your quarterback must find a comfortable position with his hands up under the center's crotch to receive the ball. He must put his hands together, with the bottom of his palms touching each other. The top hand should be his throwing hand. While pressing his bottom palms together, he should bring his bottom thumb over his top one and spread his hands apart as far as he can. At the snap, he should keep his top hand pressed firmly on the crotch as the ball hits his hand. The bottom hand must quickly ride up as it grips the ball. Then in a quick motion, the quarterback steps back with the football and starts the play. This process should be practiced until it is second nature between the QB and center. Repetition. Repetition.

Running Backs - From the beginning of summer drills teach all your running backs how to receive a hand-off. On the side the quarterback gives the ball to the running back is considered the back's inside. So it's inside arm up chest high (palm down) and the outside arm across the stomach (palm up). Once the ball is placed in the RB's stomach, both arms close like a vice and the running back is on his way.

To practice holding on to the football, have your running backs run between rows of players with shield pads who bump and slap at the football as they jog through.

Blocking techniques for running backs is similar to that of offensive linemen. Engage blocking. Cut blocking. Kick out blocking and of course pass protection.

Carioca drills are for hip flexibility and foot movement. (In carioca, the player runs down the line, keeping his arms stretched out horizontal and parallel to line. Then he crosses the left foot behind the right foot and plants it on the ground. The right foot comes back across the left foot back to a ready position, and then he crosses the left foot in front of the right foot and alternately then reverses his steps down the line.)

Agility ladder drills. (Ladder drills can be

chalked squares on the ground resembling two ladders side by side, a foot or more apart or roped squares 12-15 inches high that resembles two ladders by side.) The player runs through the ladders with his head straight ahead, placing a foot in each square without touching the chalk or rope.

Tight End – There are multiple drills for the tight end position. The blocking technique is quite similar that of offensive line. Engage and drive. Cut blocks. And pass protection. Carioca drills. Agility ladder drills. TE must also catch the football. They must practice inside and clean releases from the line of scrimmage on pass plays to avoid being jammed up by linebackers.

Split End and Flanker – Drills for these positions include running precise pass routes. Carioca drills. Agility ladder drills. Separating from man coverage. Finding an open area in zone coverage. Downfield blocking techniques. And, of course, catching the football.

DEFENSIVE DRILLS AND TECHNIQUES

Linemen – Basic run stopping, pass rushing and tackling drills. Hitting the dummy sled, bouncing off then spinning off to the next dummy pad is good for balance and getting back on their feet after being knocked down. Two on two linemen pit drills will sharpen engagement and shedding blocks skills. Practice arm swerves and swimming techniques for rushing the passer. Carioca drills. Agility ladder drills.

—- A balanced 3 or 4 point stance with staggered heel to toe with opposite foot. Keep shoulders and butt level. At the snap, raise hands quickly to shed blocks. If unblocked in the gap, watch for pulling or trapping linemen. If double teamed, use strength to fight through it or subtly grab a piece of one or both offensive linemen and drop to the ground to clog up the hole. In pass rushing, use speed and hands to blow through or go around the blocker.

Linebackers – Basic run stopping, pass rushing and tackling drills. The tip drill to help in catching interceptions.

Carioca drills. Back peddling and lateral movement drills for chasing down sweeps and options plus helps for dropping into man and zone pass coverage. Agility ladder drills.

Cone drills.

—Outside backer: Two point standing up.

Keep a low center of gravity. Stay a yard or two outside the tight end or tackle. On short yardage, goal line or special calls, line up on tight end's shoulder and jam him at the snap. Keep outside containment. Use hands and arms freely.

—Inside backer: Stands about 4-5 yards off the line of scrimmage. (2-3 yards on short yardage defense) A two point stance with knees bent in a crouch position. Hands out and ready to strike. Quickly attack assigned gap at the snap or flow laterally down the line to the football or step back into pass coverage.

Cornerbacks - Basic run stopping and tackling drills, especially open field tackling. Back peddling drills. Carioca drill. Agility ladder drills. Tip drill. Pass coverage drills. Press, man to man coverage drills.

—Two point standing up. Man to man: lines up on the receiver in front of him and follows receiver if he goes in motion. Plays to the inside of receiver and forces him to the outside. Zone: drops back and covers appropriate area of the field. Supports runs (especially QB options) around the end and forces runners inside.

Safeties - Basic run stopping and tackling drills, especially open field tackling. Back peddling drills. Carioca drill. Agility ladder drills. Tip drill. Pass coverage drills. Press, man to man coverage drills.

—Two point standing up. Lines up 15-18 yards from the line of scrimmage. Strong Safety keys the tight end and cheats up towards the line of scrimmage on certain defensive calls. Free Safety helps cornerbacks with deep passes closes down on sweep runs around the end.

REPETITION

The dog days of summer practices and practices during the regular season are for practicing. So, practice. Don't be afraid to practice hard and practice often. And never fear repetition. Practice is doing the same thing over and over again, maybe varying it from play to play, from day to day and week to week. However, during the summer, there is no next opponent. Repetition is your next opponent. To learn a craft is to practice it. And many times you practice it over and over.

One day during summer practice, my head coach at my high school was not pleased with how the center and left guard failed to execute the double team block on the defensive tackle. So he ran the same play calling for the center/guard double team block seven consecutive times. On the seventh play, the center and guard finally rooted out the defensive tackle with flawless execution. Some may call what my coach did a bit extreme. I don't. I call it practice. If the center and guard had left that practice session without defeating the defensive tackle that practice would have been in vain, thus useless and meaningless for them and the entire team. That's what practice is for, to practice. Don't be afraid of repetition.

PRACTICE DURING THE SEASON

Once you enter the regular season your practice session structure will change. So, it is wise to incorporate parts of your summer drills into your new practices. For high school coaches, I would suggest for a Friday game that you use Sunday afternoon for game film meeting.

On Mondays continue working on drills in

position units. By now, good technique should be second nature to your players. Continue to work on it at least three times a week at the beginning of Monday, Tuesday and Wednesday practices.

Most young people can remember what they do easier than what someone else does. So, work your practices to that frame. Spend the last 30-40 minutes of Monday and the first part of Tuesday (after your drills session) going over your team's game plan for your next opponent. Full and half speed scrimmages or even walk through should suffice. The last part of the Tuesday session start going over your opponents plays against your offense and defense in full scrimmages. Note and address any key players, key plays and key situations pertaining to your opponent.

Most of Wednesday should be devoted to this as well. Remember to stress constant repetition and reacting to your opponents tendencies. The last part of Wednesday should be focused on special teams. Just because you're into the regular season there's no reason to start ignoring this facet of the game. Practice all phases of the kicking game for a good 25-35 minutes.

On the day before the game, many coaches like to run a light practice. No pads. Just helmets and cleats. That's fine but still make it a serious practice. Without pads do not mean slacking off of intensity. Again, go over your opponents tendencies, both offensive and defensive. Make sure your walkthroughs are crisp and precise. Then briefly go over your game plan. Then it's special teams time. For this you can run full speed. Sprints, long snaps, holding, kickoffs, onside kickoffs and field goals for distance and accuracy. Now is the time for your kicker to show his teammates the fruits of his week's labor.

MID-SEASON BREAK IN PRACTICE ROUTINE

A high school regular season usually consists of nine or ten games, a game each week. Junior high, middle school, recreational and pee wee leagues have fewer games. At sometime during the season, your team is going to need a break from the daily regular practice routine. If there is an open date in the middle of your schedule, take advantage of it. You might want to run light drills during that week or even take a few days off to allow your players to get away from football.

Most teams do not have an open date on the schedule, thus have a game every week. However, if you discover or sense that your team would benefit from a day off, by all means, take a break. As I mentioned earlier young people need structure and a sense of routine in their lives. However, from time to time, we all need to deviate from our normal activities. Gauge your team. Monitor them. Maybe your squad has suffered a couple of close heartbreaking losses, or worse yet, maybe they've been blown out in back to back games. A change of pace would do you and them good. One way is to change your schedule. Take a Monday off. Or make it a weight training day. Or run a light practice, just helmets and shoes. If you had a horrific last game, consider not showing the video of that game. Or maybe burn it. Then on Tuesday focus on your next opponent. Another change of pace is to throw a party (get-together) for your players, cheerleaders and parents right after a Wednesday or Thursday practice. It should last just an hour or so to chat with parents and maybe give an update on the team's progress and hopes for the remainder of the season. Gestures like these could be just the boost your squad needs to charge into the second part of the season with more determination and focus.

SCOUTING OTHER TEAMS

The scouting of other teams has always been an important part of football, since the beginning of football itself. Knowing what types of plays your next opponent runs is quite beneficial. Instead of scouting plays, you're mostly looking for tendencies. Tendencies are what a team does in certain situations. A team most likely will not always run the same play in a similar game situation, but they will, however, most likely, run similar plays and with their best player. Usually in high school and recreational levels of football scouting a team's best players may be your best option. You need to know where they are on the field (especially in crucial situations) at all times. Also remember to scout a team's special teams units. At this level of football, many teams get quite creative with this phase of the game. Don't get fooled and get burned on a gadget play. Be prepared!!!

NINE
IN-GAME STRATEGIES

SITUATIONS

Let me be clear. Your team should always play to its strength. An old saying says: "do what you do best". *Sam Rotigliano, former head coach of the Cleveland Browns once said before a big game, "We don't worry about what the other team is going to do. We'll do what we do best".*

If your team is a primarily running team, then by all means you should run the football, and run it often. At the same token, if you're a passing team, throw the ball.

However, football is a game of situations and a game of adjustments. To be successful, you'll need to be able adjust to various situations that arise on the field in a game. For a running team, third down and 12 yards to go will be somewhat difficult to convert. Third and 12 is considered a passing down. Maybe not for running powerhouses like Nebraska, Oklahoma or Texas of 40 years ago, but most teams, including those in the NFL, need to pass on third down and 12 yards to go and so will you.

Ironically, for the passing squad, a third and 3 or fourth and two yards to go can pose extreme difficulties, as well as being near the goal line or starting a drive inside the 20. Usually on short yardage situations or near the goal line, defenses will blitz everyone including the water boy. You must be able to convert short yardage or make the third down and long. Be versatile. Be flexible. Execute your strengths and your weaknesses will be few. It's easier said than done. But that's what practice is for. Good teams will try to take away your strengths and force you out of your game. Surprise them and be effective in all facets of the game. As head coach, it is your responsibility to make your weaknesses work in your favor.

If you are a running team, you *must* find those pass plays that your quarterback is comfortable with. Use pass plays that your offense can execute with confidence and efficiency. *Screen passes* can be easy to execute. *Flair passes* to a running back in the flats will work. *Curl pattern passes* gives your quarterback a stationary target to hit and usually a clear one against a zone defense. *Fly and post patterns* are good for quarterbacks with strong arms but with little touch or control. Let them air it out.

If your quarterback is not comfortable running the ball, most rules of thought are don't have him run. I disagree. A player at a skilled position should be able to perform all tasks demanded of him for the team's success. Here are a few ways to get your QB running the football with a modicum of success and confidence.

First have him run quarterback sneaks; not just in short yardage or goal line situations, but run sneaks on any down when there is a large gap in the defensive line over the center. Second, have him run predetermined QB sweeps or option plays. On the options, he's either going keep the football and turn it up field, or he's going to pitch the ball no matter what defense he encounters. This eliminates the pressure of having to make a split-second decision on the field. When your quarterback becomes more familiar and adept with the option play, or when he gets tired of getting smacked by the defensive end, he'll become more efficient. Then run a few bootlegs. Faking a handoff in one direction and running the other way with open field in front of him is a great confidence builder for running the ball.

Believe it or not, handing off the football can cause high anxiety in a lot of quarterbacks. Make handing the ball off simple. No reverse pivots coming from center. Have your QB just turn to the side he's going to hand off the ball. No veers or reaching handoffs. Calling a draw play allows the throwing QB his natural motion of dropping back then he simply turns and gives the ball to the waiting running back. A direct snap to a running back will always ease a quarterback's mind. Remember, comfort is the key. If your quarterback is settled down and confident, your offense has an excellent opportunity to do well on every play. Make your quarterback comfortable.

If your offensive line isn't a good pass-blocking unit, keep a back or two in the backfield to help out with pass protection. Rolling your quarterback out of the pocket is an excellent way to take the pressure off your offensive line. Sustaining blocks on the move will help them push defenders and/or even get in a few cut blocks. Run play-action pass plays. This will allow your O-linemen to take advantage of hesitant defensive linemen who may go for the fake hand-off. On three-step quick passes, the offensive line will be able to fire out forward and quickly engage the defensive line before they can get in pass rush mode.

For pass-happy teams, going play-action is just a waste of motion. Faking the run has no effect if you rarely run the football and/or if you haven't run the ball effectively all game. An offensive line that has difficulties with run blocking can be helped in a number of ways. Here are some techniques you can use to instill run blocking confidence:

—Draw plays allow the O-line to pass block on a running play.

—Sweeps and tosses around the ends allow your offensive line to ride block without fully engaging defenders.

—Quick runs up the middle with the fullback allows your line to fire out quickly and not have to hold blocks as long as they would on a slower developing plays.

—Lastly, you can have your linemen slant block to the left or right. Engage and drive or just ride the defender in the direction he's going. The easier you make the blocking, the better success even a throwing offense will have at controlling the line of scrimmage.

DOWN AND DISTANCE

Down and distance is the major dictator of any coach's play calling decisions. What part of the field a team is operating from also greatly influences what play is called.

When on offense the football field can be dissected into six parts: *Danger*, *Caution*, *Go*, *4th down*, *Attack* and *Score*.

(See fig. 9-1)

Danger – From your goal line to your 20 yard line. You want to run your best and basic running plays or a screen pass in this area of the field.

Caution – In your territory from the 20 yard line to your 40 yard line. You can open up your playbook a bit more. Sweeps and basic off-tackle run plays. Screens, flats, curls and deep out passes.

Go – Between your 40 and your opponent's 40 yard line. Take charge. Run and pass at will. Even maybe use a gadget play or two. Just keeping moving the chains.

4th down – Inside your opponent's 35 to their 20 yard line. On any 4th and shorts, go

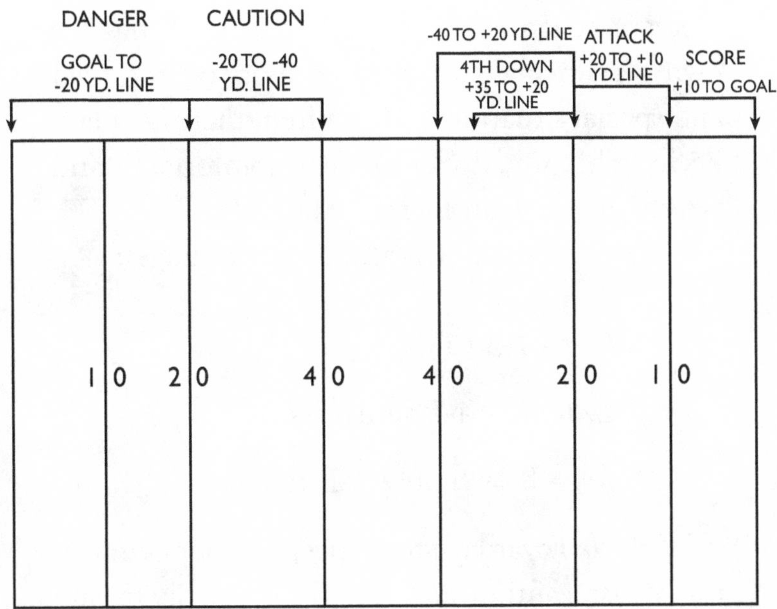

FIG. 9-1

for the first down. If you have a good kicker, the kick field goals.

Attack – Inside the 20 to the 10 yard line. The field is getting shorter. Pass the football!!

Score – Inside the 10 yard line to the end zone. With less than 30 feet to the end zone, you must use your best running and passing plays. Don't forget about your tight end in this area of the field.

Every coach at every level of football has his own certain plays for various spots on the field and special situations. Most often, there are plays he feels his squad can execute comfortably and yet efficiently. Run them.

Here are some down and distance gauges:

***Short* - 1-3 yards to go;

***Midrange* - 4-7 yards to go;

***Long* - 8 or more yards to go;

With ***short*** yardage to go deep in your own territory, use caution and run the football. In any other area of the field, your entire playbook is open to you. ***Midrange*** yards to go for a first down can cause a few problems even though you may be enjoying some success on the field. Four to seven yards may seem like a short distance but deep in your own territory it can feel like a mile. In this situation, a screen pass might catch the defense in a blitz or dropping into pass coverage. A quick dive with the fullback could surprise the defense. Other plays that could garner a first down are a quarterback bootleg, a quick slant pass or a flanker reverse. Again, if you are not deep in your own territory, open up your playbook.

Long yardage to go for a first down is just that, long. However, eight or more yards to pick up are quite manageable. If your team is down by 14 points in the fourth quarter and facing third down and 20 yards to go, running a 34 Isolation is not going to advance your situation. Give yourself the opportunity to pick up the yardage. Throw the football! Throw crossing routes, curl and go, post, fly or even a screen, but pick up the first down. Keep the drive alive. Be aggressive.

Call your plays according to how your team has been performing. If you've been running the ball effectively, by all means keep calling running plays. Likewise, if you've been passing the ball well, continue to pass it.

If your team has struggled throughout a game, continue to call the few plays that have worked and some of your best plays from practice earlier in the week.

TEN

GETTING BLOWN OUT AND BLOWING OUT OTHERS

Sometimes the action on the field won't go your way. Either your team was not ready to play, your squad committed a lot of turnovers or the other team was just better than your team or maybe even all three. At some time or another every team gets blown out of a game.

If your team is losing by five touchdowns in the fourth quarter, there's a good chance that you're not going to win the game. This situation can easily lead to poor sportsmanship, sloppy execution and worst of all, injuries. Don't let that happen. You should set goals during the blowout. Make it a game within a game, if you will. Challenge your offense to score two touchdowns and/or challenge your defense to hold the opposition scoreless for the rest of the game and/or force a turnover. Your team should realize that things will not always good their way, no matter how good a team is. However, they are expected to play full tilt until the final gun.

At the same token, there will be times where your

squad will hand out butt whippings. Don't allow your players to get caught up in humiliating their opponents. With the game well in hand, use this valuable game time for scrimmaging. Focus and execution are still vitally important. First, you want to stay consistent. Break the huddle with authority and jog to the line of scrimmage. Your quarterback should bark out signals as if it's the first plays of the game, strong and with confidence. Second, run crisp plays 100%. Third, remember your sportsmanship. If your team is winning 42-10 with five minutes left to play, there is no need for your guys to talk smack. You have proven your superiority and dominance for over three quarters. Show some class, and finish out the game clean.

The conventional thought in coaching circles is that you don't run up the score on an opponent. I don't subscribe to that train of thought. However, let me be clear. I don't think coaches should intentionally run up the score, but sometimes it is inevitable and unavoidable. I subscribe to playing hard and trying to win until the final gun. Let me explain further: Let's say that your team is ahead 42-0 at the beginning of the 4th quarter. It just makes sense that you pull your starters and regulars out of the game and let your back-up players play in the final quarter. On large high school teams, the second and third or even 4th string guys rarely get the opportunity to play. So let them play. Let them play hard and all out. Your opponents, at this juncture of the contest, probably may still have some of their starters and regulars in the game. They are most likely are fighting hard to keep from getting shut out. (I'm sure they have "getting blown-out goals" just as you do.) So your team should play hard as well.

In 1983, the University of Nebraska beat the University of Minnesota 84-13. Golden Gopher's head coach, Joe Salem, accused the Cornhuskers of running up the score on them. Legendary Nebraska head coach, Tom Osborne, countered by saying that he can't help if Salem's team couldn't stop his third and fourth string players from scoring. I agree with Coach Osborne. It's not your fault that your opponents cannot stop your second and third string reserves. Your players should not have to lie down, roll over, not score or play light defense just because you are blowing out the opposing team. My attitude is that there is no such thing as running up the score. Each team should play hard until 0:00 shows on the clock, no matter what the score is. Another important reason to play 100% with a big lead is to avoid injuries. The moment a player does not hustle 100% on each play, that's the moment he gets hurt. Each play should be played to the fullest until the whistle blows.

ELEVEN
MAKING THE GRADE AND PAMPERING PLAYERS

GRADES

There's and old saying that goes like this: "There are some things in life you can't compromise." Grades are one of those things. Integrity, accountability and priorities come before wins and losses. There is absolutely no way you can demand excellence from your players, motivate them or lend advice if you don't hold their feet to the fire when it comes to grades in the classroom.

Most, if not all, high school districts across the country have made a passing grade in the classroom a prerequisite for even participating in any sport. That's great. Unfortunately, many coaches fudge on this requirement citing various reasons which I call excuses. Don't be one of those coaches.

There is a list of excuses some coaches use. One of the most common excuses for ignoring the rules is that a certain player(s) is the main cog in the team's wheel. And that the wheel can't turn without the cog in question. I say fix the wheel by having that player(s) make the grade or squeak on without the player(s).

Another excuse is "We can't compete if he doesn't (or they don't) play." That's insulting to the other players on the team. Think about it. The team isn't capable of competing if one or two players don't play in a game. Football is a team game. As long as you have eleven players on your team, you can compete. Here's another excuse; "Well, he's not a bright guy. Don't take away the only thing he knows and does well". Again, that's quite insulting to that player, as a person. I'm sure his parents would not appreciate that comment, especially coming from his head coach.

More excuses. "This is the biggest game of the season". And of course, the game that the star player is going to miss is *always* the "biggest game of the season". And finally, this the most disgusting excuse of them all. "He has a terrible home life, and football might be the only way he makes it out of his neighborhood." That excuse sickens me because it grossly assumes that the gray matter between that player's ears is not functional at all. That's not just another excuse. That's downright thoughtless. I have only two words for that garbage. Bull shit!

Granted, some excuses may have a hint of

validity to them, but they are still not acceptable. Life has rules, and sometimes the rules don't seem fair. Life isn't fair all the time, and the teenage years are a great time in life to learn just that.

If a kid has to use a wheelchair or he has wooden leg, he would be physically unable to play football. At the same token, if a physically capable student does not make the minimum grade requirements, he has rendered himself mentally (academically) unable to play football. And he should not be allowed to participate in any other extracurricular school activities until his grades are up to par. Tell your players to go to class and do the classroom assignments so they can play football. That seems simple enough. As head coach, you must strictly adhere to these principles no matter how detrimental it is to your team.

TEAMMATES

Like making a key block that springs a running back for a 60 yard run or a defensive lineman taking on two offensive linemen to free up a linebacker to make a tackle, your players should support one another in the classroom as well. Impress upon your team that teammates help each other to remain grade-eligible. Players who are earning "A" or "B" grades in the classroom should be encouraged to tutor those who need to pull up their grades. A little academic help may be just what's needed for a player to succeed in the classroom.

Every player is vital to your team's success, so each player needs to take responsibility to remain on the team for the entire season. Insist that each of your players take their responsibilities seriously. Football is a team sport. Each player and coach has to keep his end of the bargain. The coaches are charged with fielding a competitive team and keeping distractions to a minimum. Players are charged with remaining competitive with a superior effort on the field and in the classroom. This means not playing the "dumb jock" role, but going to class, studying, turning in assignments. True teammates won't let bad grades and unacceptable classroom behavior derail the team's continuity. You are the coach. Take charge! Outline your academic expectations to your team from day one.

Having a study hall for players an hour or so just before or just after practice can be quite beneficial. Bringing in school tutors is always a good idea.

If a player does not conform to your standards,

release him from your team and implore him to begin to improve his attitude and disposition. Don't abandon the player once he is no longer on your team. Assist him with whatever situations or problems he has that are preventing him from succeeding in the classroom. If grades are a problem, find him a tutor. If he's has trouble socially, advise him to seek counsel in a school counselor, a favorite teacher, his clergyman and/or, of course, his parents.

PAMPERING PLAYERS

In most high schools, football is biggest moneymaking sport it has. That being the case, there are some people outside of the game such as school administration, city boosters, parents and other interested parties who may tend to coddle, pamper or inappropriately assist players, "star" players. Reasons for such attention vary from each individual. Interested parties may even offer your players gifts, perks or special favors. I call all this special attention to certain players simply another distraction. As mentioned in the previous chapter, it is your job to minimize such distractions, or in this case eliminate them. Check with your state high school athlete commission and your school to see what the rules are with respect of players receiving and accepting gifts and favors. (This is rarely a problem with recreational, junior high or pee wee football leagues.) You must tell your players what is appropriate and what is not appropriate concerning on how to deal with outside influences. Let them know where you stand. The only way you can give your football program the dignity and respect it deserves is to create an aura of credibility in every facet of your actions. You must tell all outside influences that your team is off-limits to any improper interest, no matter how well-meaning. Your forthrightness will ultimately show your community that your staff and players at are above reproach.

Football players should not be pampered, treated like royalty, or paraded around like prized cattle. Players should be expected to bear the responsibilities like any other student, like any other citizen. It's good if others admire your athletes and respect their God-given talent and skills. However, they should be given the same deference for being decent human beings.

TWELVE
MOTIVATION AND ADVICE

Young people need motivation almost on a daily basis. As head coach, your job is to motivate. Motivate them for excellence on the field. It's the off the field motivation and giving advice that can cause problems. The lives of children are influenced and shaped by the people and things they come in contact with; parents, teachers, coaches, community people, television shows, etc. That is a fact. And all that is well and good.

However, beware of the downside. The biggest problem with influencing and advising kids is that it could create conflicts with the values of the parents. Always be mindful that parents are the main "influencers", if you will, in their children's lives. Giving advice is fine. Getting involved can cause problems.

Being involved with children who aren't your own can be like walking a tight rope without a safety net below. On the one hand, since you are the head coach, society almost demands that you be a role model. On the other hand, you are not allowed to be too intimate or overly concerned about, or involved in, your players' personal lives. Given that, you must resist the urge to try to fix your players or any issues they may have. If a player comes to you with a serious personal problem, direct him to the best and appropriate person who can properly assist him. Most often, being a role model is just being yourself and doing your job and being the best head coach you can be. And if a kid sees that and wants to be like you, then that's fine and dandy. That's the best motivation and influencing you can give anyone.

THIRTEEN
NON-FOOTBALL PERSONNEL

SCHOOL ADMINISTRATION AND BOOSTERS

I don't think much of politicizing the game of football. In fact, I see football and politics as oil and water, or an oxymoron. They don't mix at all. However, that won't stop people from trying to make them a match made in heaven, and it won't stop them from trying to have a stake in your team, especially if you have a good football program and/or your team is doing well on the field. If you're a successful, sometimes you can't get around it. It seems that everybody wants to be associated with a winner. Many high schools and recreational leagues have boosters, very involved parents or even success-driven principals and or sometimes school district officials up the food chain. I think that can be a good thing. As a coach, you always want to stay in contact with those interested in your team's well-being. And if your team is doing well, you might have contact with mayor of your town or other city or even regional officials. With all that being said, boosters, parents and interested others are a secondary concern for you. You are the head man in charge of your team. You should only run your team the way "you" see fit. The pressures and influences of interested parties can be, at times, quite intimidating. It is not unheard for parents to pressure coaches to get more playing time for their "little darlings". I'm confident that in 90% of high school football societies, pressures of this nature are rare and mostly non-existent. However, if you do experience unusual outside pressures and influences concerning your team, you must stand your ground. Don't let it disrupt your team.

CHEERLEADERS

Cheerleaders are a special clan. Whenever your team needs a physical, emotional or psychological boost they are always there to your team's rescue. Be especially kind and grateful to them and their director. As you will quickly discover, these human balls of enthusiasm and energy are your truest and most loyal fans. Cheerleaders will cheer for your team when you're trailing 38-0 late in the 4th quarter with the other team driving for another touchdown. At many points during the season you'll want to harness and bottle that optimism of these young people, and let your entire team drink from that bottle.

Try to stay involved in your school cheerleaders' off-the-field activities. Always have a few senior players attend their fundraisers such as car washes, bake sales, etc. Remember to thank them for just being there on the sidelines for each game. Invite them to special team events, such as those mid-season breaks from practice we discussed earlier in chapter 8, weekend team activities and honor them, as well, at the end of the season banquet.

FOURTEEN
A COACH'S PHILOSOPHY AND OVERVIEW

At every level, football is the ultimate team sport. Eleven guys on the field, each with different duties and responsibilities to produce a positive outcome every 35-40 seconds. It's a physical game and at times a brutal one. Discipline plays a huge part of the game of football. Discipline breeds consistency. Consistency leads to nearly flawless execution. And execution leads to success.

Each coach must take the time to evaluate his team with a fine tooth comb. It is up to the head coach to find the proper personnel to fit every position on the field. It is up to you to know the things your team is capable of doing well and the things they don't do as well. Then constantly work on the things they don't do well. There is nothing more frustrating than to watch a primarily running team fall behind by three or four touchdowns then start throwing the football without any idea of how the passing game works. Let's face it. It's easier to run the ball than it is to pass it. Nevertheless, as a head coach, your job is to make your team proficient in all facets of the game. You might be a wishbone, triple option, veer type of running team, but that shouldn't mean that you are not able to progress efficiently down the field by throwing the football. As head coach, it is your obligation to give your team every opportunity to win.

Countless times I have seen high school and lower level recreational teams totally neglect the kicking part of the game. This archaic attitude of going for it of fourth down instead of kicking a field goal; or going for the two-point conversion instead of kicking the extra-point; or having a lineman or your best athlete as a kicker is a piss-poor excuse for not having a legitimate kicker. At the high school level, this is an easy problem to solve. First, work with that player who wants to be a kicker and shows potential to be a decent kicker. Work with him everyday. Chances are that you'll have a diamond-in–the-rough who just needs a bit of polishing. Or find a kid on the soccer team and have him just kick footballs at every practice. At lower levels of football, the task of finding a kicker may be more challenging. Most likely your kicker will be a position player. Make sure you spend extra time with him before and after practice.

I realize that many high schools and organized lower levels of football have small roster sizes and an even small number of athletes (better skilled players). The temptation to only play those players is great, but I urge coaches not to settle for that. Take the time to evaluate each member of your team to see how he can contribute. *For example, when I was in high school, we had a couple of guys on the team who didn't look a bit athletic at all. Their equipment hung on them unevenly and loosely like rags on a hanger. And both were slow as molasses. However, our coaches discovered though evaluation that one was and exceptional long-snapper and the other guy seemed to sweat super glue on his palms and became a good wide receiver. Unfortunately, we didn't throw the ball much back then, but when we did, "ole glue hands" caught everything thrown his way.*

In evaluating your talent you will find just who is suited for offense or defense. You may discover that a kid is an aggressive tackler but a poor blocker or vice versa. Every quarterback or running back is not automatically a good defensive back or linebacker. Now by all means, if you have a stud of an athlete or a versatile guy who can effectively play on both sides of the football, use him that way. But make a conscious effort to utilize as many players on your roster as you can. For good team morale and continuity, put those kids who don't play much or at all on special teams whenever possible. Keep alert. Who knows? You might find a good special teams man who could fill a position if needed. One more word about special teams. Please, please, please. Practice special teams. Not just on the day before a game but everyday. And just don't go through the motions. Many games are decided by special teams play. Have your team ready to win!!!

Those coaches with larger roster sizes have an added advantage. If you are one those coaches, use that advantage by emphasizing each unit's importance. Having a meeting with offense and defense separately is a start. Have offensive, defensive and special team goals and rewards. Take the offensive line or just seniors to dinner at least twice a season. Most of all have a special relationship with your quarterbacks. In this age of super stars at every position, the quarterback is still the most important position on the field. If you make him feel comfortable and extra special, the rewards can be many. Your interaction with him should run the gambit of being his best friend to being his worst nightmare. Instilling confidence and understanding can make the most mediocre quarterback quite efficient. Don't underestimate this.

And finally, a sense of tradition is very important, if not for a team's success but for its psyche. Emphasize the relevance and importance of teams and players of the past, past coaches and memorable games. Stress and emphasize pride in the school, school colors and neighborhood pride. Revel in the importance of rivalry games and past league or conference championships and how special it is to be part of your particular team. For those high schools all ready with a rich heritage this task is easy to accomplish. For those schools or organizations with faded, unsuccessful or even non-existent traditions, the task is more difficult. However, it can be fun and a challenge to implement and commence new traditions. Keep in mind that high school is the highest level of football that will be achieved by the vast majority of kids. Help them enjoy it.

FIFTEEN

A FEW BASIC RULES AND PENALTIES

Football rules differ from state to state and city to city, however, many rules are similar. Here are some basic rules for high school, junior high and pee wee football leagues.

HIGH SCHOOL AND JUNIOR HIGH SCHOOL FOOTBALL RULES

Length of game: High school games have four quarters. Each quarter is only 12 minutes in duration. Eight-minute quarters are played for junior high games.

Kickoff: For both levels, the ball is placed at the 40 yard line of the kicking team.

Touchbacks: Any kicks (kickoffs, punts and missed field goals) that cross the goal line are considered a touchback.

The opposing team takes possession of the ball at their 20-yard line.

Pass Interference: The pass interference penalty in football is 15 yards and an automatic first down. The penalty is assessed from the line of scrimmage. It is not assessed at the spot of the foul.

Point(s) after touchdown (PAT): The team on defense may not return a blocked PAT attempt, a fumble or an interception.

Overtime: Overtime rules for both levels vary widely from state to state. Sudden death, full overtime periods and automatic tie rules appear in different areas of the country.

PEE WEE LEAGUE FOOTBALL RULES

Youth football rules are modified from those of professional, college and even football with adjustments made to provide a greater emphasis on safety for young players.

Game Rules

Pee Wee league football usually uses rules similar to high school football with some variations by region. Common penalties include holding, offside and pass interference. After a touchdown is scored, only two-point conversions are allowed instead of kicking a PAT.

Length of Game

Pee wee football rules suggest four quarters of play lasting eight minutes. The clock is stopped according to the high school rule book or may run continuously. A two-minute rest period is given between each quarter with a 10-minute halftime intermission. In most cases, if pee wee football games are unable to be completed due to weather or external circumstances, the game is declared complete if more than one half has been played.

Mercy Rule

The mercy rule is employed to avoid youth football games becoming significantly one-sided. The theory is that neither team benefits from a game with a lopsided score. In some states, if a team is leading by three or more touchdowns going into the fourth quarter, a running clock goes in effect. And also in some leagues, a game can be ended if the score deficit goes higher than a predetermined number.

Equipment

Players are forbidden to take the field in pee wee football without mandated protective equipment. Helmet, shoulder pads, hip, thigh and knee padding and must be worn at all times when playing. All equipment will be inspected beforehand by a referee. Mouth guards must also be worn, and cleats must be rubber and molded in order for a player to take the field.

Defensive Formations

No more than six defensive players may be on the line of scrimmage before the snap. Blitzing is not allowed inside the tight end or against formations where the tight end is not on the field. This is done to reduce the difficulty for offensive linemen when figuring out who to block. Any violation of this rule results in a 15-yard penalty and an automatic first down.

Kicking Situations

Coaches must declare when they're going to kick. The defense is not allowed to rush the kicker. These rules are in place for the safety of players and also to help younger kickers gain experience without the pressure encountered at higher levels.

Returning of a Kicked Ball

Only players who are under the backfield position weight limit are allowed to return a kicked ball. This rule also affects how players line up in a kicking situation. During punts, only the return man is allowed to line up deeper than 5 yards from the line of scrimmage. During kickoffs, that limit is increased to 35 yards for non-return men. If a player who is not the return man catches the ball past the 35 yard limit, the play is blown dead. In the event of a short kick, including an onside kick, weight restrictions are waived and anyone on the returning team may return the ball.

Age and Weight Limits

Pee Wee football includes age and weight limit. These regulations are in place to aid development by ensuring that players compete against other players of a similar age and weight and also to ensure their physical safety. If you're coaching pee wee league football, check with your state and local recreation authorities for proper age and weight requirements.

ABOUT THE AUTHOR

Perry Gilmore is a free-lance writer and former high school football coach. Born and raised in Battle Creek, Michigan, Gilmore graduated from Michigan State University with an interest in sports journalism. Gilmore began his football career as a reporter covering football games for the local paper, a job that led to becoming a radio and TV announcer and high school football coach. Gilmore is also the author of three screenplays and is currently working on his first novel.

CPSIA information can be obtained
at www.ICGtesting.com
Printed in the USA
BVHW040526010622
638589BV00001B/62

9 781936 185849